A Day Is Too Long

A Day Is Too Long: Reclaiming Hope and Meaning in the Face of Adversity

by

Sunny Elem

"Scripture quotations are taken from the New World Translation of the Holy Scriptures (2013 Revision)."

ISBN:

eBook: 979-8-90224-150-8

Paperback: 979-8-90224-130-0

Hardback: 979-8-90224-131-7

Published by:
Authors Publishing House
178 Broadway, 3rd Floor, #1343
New York, NY 10001, USA

Main Line: (855) 624-0155
Email: support@authorspublishinghouse.com

Table of Contents

Dedication

For those who have known the weight of a long day—

the silent battles,

the private tears,

the victories no one applauds.

For every heart that learned to stand again in the aftermath of its own breaking, and for every soul that whispered, *"I will try once more."*

May these words meet you with gentleness, shorten your weary hours, and lead you toward the One who carries what we cannot.

"May Jehovah be praised, who daily carries our load." — **Psalm 68:19**

Acknowledgments

To my family, friends, and mentors who stood by me through sleepless nights and early mornings: thank you. Your encouragement, wisdom, and feedback brought these pages to life. Your prayers gave me hope during the hardest moments. I am deeply grateful for your support.

To my wonderful wife, Franca Elem: Thank you for your unshakable support and constant love. You trusted me long before a single word was written. I remember one evening at our cluttered desk when you gave me a quiet nod of encouragement. It pierced through the noise of self-doubt. You saw promise in this endeavor when it was only a thought. You believed when my own faith wavered. Your strength served as my stabilizer. Every page bears your touch.

To my children, Precious, Chinazom, and Cherish: Thank you for staying by my side. You were there when I struggled. Your quiet support and love helped me endure.

To every reader holding this book: Your courage brings these words to life. Thank you for facing your story, rising after setbacks, and moving forward on hard days. Every small step honors your strength. Trust your journey, knowing hope and brighter days are ahead.

Finally, to the One who brings hope to broken places: This journey exists because You held me fast, Jehovah God. Your steadfast love was my beacon when I felt lost. Your guidance led my pen and heart. When I faced uncertainty, Your Word brought light. One scripture especially steadied my spirit: "For I well know the thought I am thinking toward you,' thoughts of peace, not calamity, to give you a future and hope." — **Jeremiah 29:11**.

Faith calmed my fears and gave my work life.

About the Author

Sunny Elem is a storyteller and speaker who explores the gentle resilience of the human heart. His work weaves faith, resilience, and everyday experience into reflective stories that invite readers to see their own lives with greater courage, clarity, and hope.

Drawing from spiritual insight, psychological understanding, and lived experience, Sunny writes for those who are rebuilding, one breath, one moment, one act of courage at a time. His pages speak to anyone seeking healing, direction, or a fresh sense of direction.

With a background in leadership, business, personal development, and faith-based services. Sunny deeply believes in second chances, silent miracles, and sometimes the hidden and uncommon power carried by ordinary people. He hopes every reader discovers that, despite being in long, difficult days, there is still a path toward meaning and restoration.

Introduction: The Burden of a Single Day

"A day is too long only when it has no purpose."

— Cornelius.

"Each day has enough of its own troubles."

— Matthew 6:34

In these pages, you will find a promise: Discover the Power of Purpose. This storybook invites you to explore how the meaning of each day brings hope and strength in adversity. Drawing on classic motivational wisdom, it aims to help anyone facing discouragement or loss find inner strength, courage, and faith. If you feel hopeless or alone, this book is your companion, reminding you that direction can lighten each day.

Before wisdom changed a life, before mornings murmured truths, two men crossed paths on an ordinary day. As Cornelius and Marius crossed the busy streets, the morning air carried the scent of distant rain. The metallic clang of a fire escape rattled in the distance, and the coffee smell drifted from a café. From that moment, the ordinary vanished.

The Young Man Who Looked Like He Was Running Out of Time

Marius carried a presence that left a persistent question in the air.

He was the sort of person you glimpse in passing, sensing a story you might never unravel.

He seemed to carry the world on his shoulders. His eyes wore a practiced smile, masking hidden battles. Beneath it, exhaustion settled deep, making every breath painful.

The Older Man Who Carried Peace Like an inseparable part

Cornelius was the opposite of Marius - not because he knew more, but because he let go of more illusions. Tall and gentle, calm but not fragile, his wisdom came from years, not burdens. His eyes showed depth. He looked like someone who endured loss and valued what remained.

Modestly dressed and moving with ease, he felt genuine.

He was the kind of man strangers trusted.

Not because he talked a lot, but because he didn't need to.

The alarm went off at 5:45 a.m., not with music, but with the same harsh sound that broke into Marius's dreams every morning. He turned it off and stared at the ceiling. Another day. Another race he never chose to run.

The rent was overdue. Unopened bills stacked up, accusing him. His credit card -months spent scraping by - reminded him of the fight. His boss's late-night email still stung: 'We need results by Friday.' He hadn't recovered from last week's work.

He sat up, rubbed his face, and felt the cold floor. Cheap instant coffee cuts sharply. His phone rang softly - utility alert, bank message, social feed of smiling faces, unlike his own.

He wasn't lazy or broken. He was drained, fatigue sank deep, where each morning brought a new deadline, not a promise.

Exhaustion and discouragement are common, especially when days lack purpose. This book shows that even a small sense of purpose - not just strength - can make days lighter, ease loneliness, and bring hope.

That morning, instead of hurrying into another hollow day, he grabbed his jacket and walked into the cold. The city was waking: buses starting, horns resounding through wet streets, strangers hurrying through never-long-enough hours.

Marius wandered until he got to a small park near his apartment. On a bench by the fountain sat an elderly man, coat buttoned, hands around a hot cup of coffee.

"You look like someone fighting tomorrow before today has even begun," the man gently said.

Marius stopped. Something about the man's voice - calm, steady, and sure - made him sit down without saying a word.

They sat in silence as the city moved: joggers, delivery bikes, a mother with a stroller - all busy with private hardships.

Marius finally spoke, his voice trembling. He paused briefly and took a shallow breath. "Every single day feels like I'm drowning under work, bills, and deadlines." He paused again and chose his next words. "It's like being slowly buried alive." His speech faltered, and he let out a quiet sigh. "Debt and disappointment squeeze me until I can barely breathe." He stopped and stared at the ground. "I wake up aching everywhere," he admitted. A touch of fragility showed. "I'm not living; I'm struggling through the hours, desperate for air."

The old man nodded. "You sound like a man trying to carry the whole day on his shoulders."

Marius frowned. "What do you mean?"

Cornelius grinned subtly, his eyes comforting but sharp with wisdom.

You say a day is too long because you try to carry it all at once. Each grief, fear, past doubt, and future worry is packed into one day. This makes the day unbearably heavy.

The words persisted. Marius stared at the ground. "Then what should I do?" he asked quietly.

Shorten your day. Don't live each day as if it were your whole life. Focus on what matters. Start small; organize your room for fifteen minutes. This brings focus and creates a gentle tone. As Marius leans back on the bench, a thought crosses his mind. Might something so simple shift the weight he carries? Is there hope, or just skepticism fighting the urge to try?

Marius leaned back on the bench, chest loosening with a fragile sigh. "It sounds simple," he spoke quietly, "but how do you even move when everything inside feels shattered?"

"The secret of peace, Marius, isn't conquering everything. It focuses on the moment and gives it a clear purpose. A day is too long only when it lacks meaning. When you choose even a small purpose, time works for you."

He paused and watched sunlight move over the fountain. Then he added softly, "Remember, when you wake up tomorrow, you don't have to fix your whole life. You only need to live today. Even then, just one moment at a time."

They sat in silence. The pigeons scattered as a kid laughed softly nearby. Somewhere, a tower bell began to ring the hour.

Marius looked around. The city - noise, debts, deadlines - remained. But inside, a change occurred. There was quiet relief. For the first time in a while, he noticed a tender possibility where once there had been weight.

Cornelius stood up and straightened his coat. "You'll be all right," he said. "Just remember to shorten the day and live it with purpose."

And with that, he walked away, fading into the morning crowd.

Marius stayed, watching the sky brighten, recalling the old man's words. He reached for his phone, not to check messages, but to type one line.

Then, with a breath that appeared like a new start, he stood up and began to walk. He didn't go fast or far, but he moved forward.

Consider the silent burden you shoulder each morning. It is a weight that dims the dawn and tilts the day's start toward sorrow. Name this burden - what weighs on you? Your pain could differ from Marius's, but it can cut as deep.

You may face loss - death, dreams ending, or betrayal. Debt, disappointment, or discouragement can sap your strength. Sometimes, struggles are hidden - anxiety, loneliness, or the battle between your public face and private pain.

If so, this book is for you.

The main truth Cornelius shared with Marius is simple: You don't have to carry all of today. You don't have to fix everything at once. Choose just one purposeful moment or task. Focus on that, rest when you need, and treat yourself with compassion. Living with purpose this way can ease guilt and unfold the burden of an overwhelming day.

That is how hope returns.

As you read these pages - from lessons about thought and faith to the courage to start over - you will walk with Marius through every question, each calm instant, and every new day. Marius does not walk a straight path. He faces moments when hope wavers, and he relapses into doubt. He learns that healing is not linear. At these times, you may see your own struggles. As you walk with him, you may find that what hurt you was never meant to define you.

The cracks that seemed like endings can become openings for light. Pain that confines you can also become a passage. It can lead to peace, purpose, and fulfillment.

By the time you finish this book, I hope you see your scars not as proof that you were broken. Let them be a map showing how you found your way home.

So, take a breath. Whatever you've lost, whatever you fear, whatever has brought you to this book, let it rest for now.

Here is your moment to shorten the day. Focus on small purposes. Even the longest hours can offer hope and beauty. Purpose, even in small actions, brings hope.

This Book Is the Story of What Happened After

It is the story of a tired young man learning to breathe again.

The story of an older man who brought hope back, not by preaching, but by asking questions, using simple images, and sharing small instances that appeared ordinary but were not.

It is a quiet story, powerful because it is simple.

A human story, special because it is honest.

Inside these pages, you will not find clichés.

You will find wisdom that meets you where life happens. Whether your pain resembles Marius's or is different, these pages recognize the uniqueness of every struggle. Each life story and all struggles are acknowledged, showing a wisdom that can transcend circumstances. You will walk with Marius as he discovers the key stages of his journey:

Ground:

- how to shorten a day
- how to face grief without breaking down or collapsing
- how to command the mind

Rebuild:

- how to rise from failure

- how to rebuild intention
- how to cultivate peace

Sustain:

- how to reclaim purpose
- how to find steadiness in a world that shakes
- how to let hope survive the night

You will hear Cornelius's voice - steady, patient, and clear - until you notice it is starting to steady something inside you too.

This Is More Than a Book: Consider It an Invitation.

Somewhere in these chapters is a sentence meant for you.

It will come gently…

quietly…

deeply…

The way truth always does.

This book will not shout.

It will walk with you, just as Cornelius walked with Marius, until the soft courage of each lesson becomes your own.

The day you've been trying to reclaim is waiting for you. Picture a morning where joy returns to your life, where pleasure peeks through the curtain of routine. Imagine sitting down for a quiet meal, enjoying every bite, not distracted by the burden of unending tasks but grateful for the moment's simplicity. Visualize a relaxing evening walk where the soft shades of dusk do not signal an end filled with dread, instead a promise of balance. These tiny scenes of your reclaimed day are within reach, giving a glimpse of the success toward which you are journeying.

Why You May Not Want to Put This Book Down

Because somewhere between the lines, you may recognize yourself:

in Marius's exhaustion

in his fear

in his grief

in his attempts to rise

in his rediscovery of promise

in his final understanding of purpose

And when a story reflects your own, it becomes impossible to turn away.

A Final Word Before You Begin

James Hadley Chase captured characters with a single incisive line. He might have summarized Marius as a young man whose eyes bore more weight than his hands. Turning to Cornelius, Chase might have said he could calm a storm with quietude. And for you, dear reader, remember that picking this book was no accident, even if its purpose remains unclear.

Turn the page.

The day you've been waiting to reclaim unfolds here.

Chapter One: Living Each Day with Meaning and Resolve

"Every man's life is a sum of days. Master the day, and you master the life."

— Cornelius.

"Teach us how to count our days so that we may acquire a heart of wisdom."

— Psalm 90:12

The First Morning of Change

The morning after his first actual conversation with Cornelius, Marius awoke before the alarm. He lay in bed, feeling the dawn's stillness, a singular tranquility washing over him. For the first time in years, the morning wasn't an adversary. Calmness settled within him, suggesting promise rather than pressure.

He remembered the old man's words.

"Shorten your day."

The sentence resounded like a key turning in a lock he had held for years but never known how to use.

He sat on the edge of his bed, feet resting on the cold floor, and did something he hadn't done in a very long time: he paused. Prayed.

He didn't reach for his phone.

He didn't check the clock.

He didn't mentally rehearse the debts, the deadlines, the disappointments, or let the first worried thoughts start their usual slow climb. "I can't do this. It's all falling apart. How will I pay it all off?"

Instead, he spoke softly, not out of habit but from a new understanding, repeating the ancient plea from **Psalm 90:12**:

"Teach me to count this day… that I may gain a heart of wisdom."

The words rested in him like warm embers finding their place.

Today would have a single focus, not a scattered war of intentions.

Today, he would choose one thing, something meaningful, and give himself fully to it.

That choice, small as it seemed, was his first victory.

Cornelius hadn't given him a lecture the day before. He had given him a new way to see things. As daylight slowly filled the room, Marius felt as if he was finally seeing his life clearly, without the usual haze.

If the introduction had been the invitation, this would have been the threshold.

He inhaled deeply.

It was time to begin.

The Philosophy of the Present

In every age, men have tried to conquer time.

They have built calendars, written five-year plans, drafted ten-year visions, and set lifelong goals that stretch past the horizon of their courage.

Yet very few, almost none, have learned to master the smallest and most important part of destiny: today.

Cornelius had earlier mentioned to him,

"A man can drown in a river only a foot deep if he fights every direction at once."

Now Marius understood. He had been fighting past, future, fear, and failure as if his entire life needed solving before breakfast.

No mind survives that weight.

The truth was painfully simple: the mind collapses under the burden of too much time. Marius felt this collapse vividly one afternoon. He was at his desk, with piles of paperwork looming and tasks stacked like an overwhelming mountain. Paralyzed due to the overwhelming amount of what needed to be done, he found himself unable to start, unable to move. The load of the future burdened him, transforming minutes into burdens. Yet, in that very stillness, it became clear: the mind collapses when it is caught in the endless web of time unorganized and unmastered.

When someone says, "I will change my life," it can feel like a mountain appears before them—steep, unforgiving, and impossible. The mind gets tired before even taking the first step.

But when he whispers, "I will change this hour," something impressive happens.

The mind stirs.

The heart steadies.

The will awakens.

Now, the task is no longer a mountain; it is just a step. Steps lead to movement. Movement builds momentum. Momentum turns into belief. Belief becomes power. And power, practiced each day quietly, shapes destiny.

This process corresponds to the habit loop: a cue that initiates a routine, followed by the reward of empowerment. By seeing each step as the cue, the resulting movement as the routine, and the momentum gained as the reward, readers can replicate this model in their lives. In accordance with this proven habit framework, mastering The Law of Present Momentum is achievable.

Belief becomes power.

And power, repeated quietly day after day, becomes destiny.

This is the foundation of success, peace, recovery, discipline, healing, and every form of inner mastery.

This is the core principle:

The Law of Present Momentum.

Cornelius had framed it with almost childlike simplicity:

"The man who directs his present moment commands his future,"

Marius repeated the line slowly, letting it settle into the unseen architecture of his mind.

He had devoted many years to losing battles before they began - not because he lacked strength, but because he tried to live entire seasons in a single morning. He tried to fix the past, predict the future, and survive the present all at once.

No wonder life had seemed unachievable.

But now, today, he focused on just one hour.

Only one purpose.

Only one clear step.

For the first time in a long while, the day did not feel overwhelming.

It felt…possible.

The Tyranny of Tomorrow

Most men fail not because they are weak, but because they are distracted by the phantom called tomorrow.

Tomorrow is the invisible thief that robs men of strength today. It murmurs, "Rest now; you'll do it later." Or worse, it quietly speaks sharply, "Why bother? You'll never finish."

The wise know that tomorrow is an illusion, a mirage seen only by those who refuse to live in the now. Tomorrow whispers promises that trick the mind into delay and inaction. For example, a man may put off paying an important bill, thinking tomorrow will provide a better opportunity.

Another might delay finishing a workout, assuming the energy or motivation will be greater tomorrow.

The old man's words from the day before stayed with Marius like an echo that persisted:

"Shorten your day."

It was a simple sentence, but now it stayed with him into the morning like a quiet mentor.

As he sat on the edge of his bed, he realized something he had never noticed before: most of his exhaustion came not from living the present day, but from fighting a hundred tomorrows at once.

Cornelius had named it perfectly: the tyranny of tomorrow.

Tomorrow had ruled Marius for years.

It told him he would fix his habits later.

Find peace later.

Start fresh later.

Heal later.

Tomorrow had always been generous with promises and stingy with delivery.

Yesterday's worries and tomorrow's anxieties had crowded into this single dawn, and Marius felt how heavy they truly were. Cornelius had spoken the truth gently, but there was steel in it:

"You are trying to carry days you do not yet own."

Scripture once had murmured the same truth in a way Marius never paid attention to:

"Do not worry about tomorrow, for tomorrow will worry about itself…"
— Matthew 6:34

Not a sermon.

Not a threat.

Just a gentle truth about the human heart:

Peace lives only in the day you are actually standing in.

Tomorrow is a mirage.

A promise that vanishes when you reach for it.

It asks you to delay your courage, postpone your discipline, and borrow anxiety you do not yet have the strength for.

Cornelius had taught him, even after knowing him for only a few minutes, that life is won not in the decades he feared, but in the days he overlooked.

And as Marius breathed in the cold, fresh morning breeze, he made a quiet vow:

Today will not be sacrificed to tomorrow.

Not again.

How the Mind Builds Momentum

Marius wasn't a new man by morning - no one changes overnight - but something inside him had moved. It seemed like a hinge had moved and a door had opened.

He felt it when he placed his feet on the floor.

He felt it when he let silence sit beside him instead of rushing to fill it.

He felt it when he spoke in a low voice, almost uncertainly:

"Just one meaningful thing…today."

A single deliberate act is the spark that wakes the mind. It's more than just a metaphor; this act releases a subtle flow of dopamine, the neurotransmitter responsible for feelings of reward and motivation. This scientific grounding reinforces the concept of the mind as a heavy wheel, initially hard to push but gaining momentum with each purposeful action. To make this personal, try a simple experiment: when you achieve a small win tomorrow morning, pause and notice how you feel. Pay attention to that sense of accomplishment and motivation, the dopamine spark that neuroscience tells us accompanies even the smallest success.

The human mind is like a weighty wheel.

Still and stubborn at first.

Hard to push.

But once moving, even slightly, it begins to help itself along.

Momentum.

Marius felt it as he stood up.

Not tentatively confident, but a possibility.

Not strength, but direction.

He remembered another gentle reality he had read long ago but never lived:

"Do not be anxious over anything, but in everything…the peace of God that surpasses all understanding will guard your heart and mental powers."**— Philippians 4:6, 7**

Peace wasn't something waiting at the finish line.

Peace arrived the moment he started moving.

So, he took a humble start. Before beginning his first task, Marius paused to take a deep breath, centering himself in the moment. This simple act reminded him of Cornelius's wisdom and helped him approach the day with purpose. He made his bed - one push.

He made a simple cup of coffee - one push.

He opened his window and let the cold, fresh morning breeze in - one push.

He decided what one meaningful thing he would give his strength to - one more push.

It was barely a beginning.

But beginnings were never meant to be dramatic.

Cornelius had said it with nearly playful certainty:

"Win this hour, and you will already sense the burden of your life shift.

Win the day, and the future will begin to obey you."

Momentum, Marius realized, was not a force the world gave him.

It acted as a force he created inside himself.

One hour at a time.

One decision at a time.

One intentional breath at a time.

As he moved through his small apartment, he felt what Cornelius meant when he compared the mind to a great wheel.

Stillness makes it heavy.

Stillness makes it stubborn.

Stillness makes it resist the very change it secretly longs for.

But if you nudge it, even just a little, something starts to change.

At first, the wheel groans.

It pushes back.

It complains that the effort is too much trouble.

But if the man pushing it persists...

If he accepts it with intention...

if he refuses to retreat from that first inch...

something notable follows:

The wheel begins to help him.

And soon, it becomes harder to stop than to continue.

Marius felt this truth in his own small beginnings.

He opened the curtains.

He softly spoke a quiet prayer, unsure though earnest.

He wrote a one-line in his journal: "Today will count."

Each action was tiny.

Scarcely a sigh.

Yet each one bore a burden greater than effort: each one created movement.

A verse he once had skimmed over suddenly returned to him:

"For who has despised the day of small beginnings?" — **Zechariah 4:10**

He finally understood what it meant.

Small beginnings are not small.

They are seeds.

They are sparks.

They are what an entire destiny can depend on.

One day of purpose strengthens belief.

Belief expands into confidence.

Confidence becomes power.

And power, repeated quietly day after day, shapes what men call destiny.

A man who wins the morning does not simply win an hour - he wins the day.

A man who wins the day begins to command his future.

Momentum is the secret every successful soul shares but rarely explains.

It transforms discipline into desire, hesitation into habit, and fear into strength.

Marius, still new to everything Cornelius had taught him, didn't yet feel powerful.

He didn't feel wise.

He didn't feel new.

But as he advanced toward the door, something inside him steadied.

The wheel had begun to turn.

Slowly.

Lightly.

Almost imperceptibly.

And for the first time in years, the resistance he felt wasn't from life pushing against him - it was from the old version of himself beginning to let go.

Thus, the man who controls the present controls his future.

This is not a theory.

It is a law.

All victory commences as a disciplined day - a day shortened to one task, one focus, one victory.

A Practical Lesson: The Shortened Day

Cornelius once said to Marius,

"You say a day is too long because you have tried to carry the whole of it at once. You have taken every sorrow, every fear, every doubt of the past and every terror of the future, and you have packed them into the next twenty-four hours. Of course, it crushes you. You are trying to lift eternity."

The remedy, he said, was simple:

Shorten your day. Do not live a day as though it were a lifetime. Live it as though it were a single task. Choose one thing that matters, and give yourself wholly to it. Ask yourself, 'Which single task tomorrow would lighten your entire week?' Direct this self-inquiry to transform Cornelius's advice into an immediate plan. For instance, you might choose to write down on paper that business idea you've been procrastinating about, write a page of your book, or organize a cluttered drawer. By visualizing specific steps, you can approach each day with clarity and purpose.

If your day feels too long, it is not time that needs changing - it is focus.

Choose one meaningful task each morning and start with something simple. It may be as small as making your bed, writing one paragraph, or calling a friend you've forgotten. Commit your whole attention to it, even if only for one hour. While focusing on this task, remember to address urgent responsibilities and necessary tasks as they arise. Integrating your chosen focus alongside these obligations will help maintain balance and reduce any anxiety about neglecting important duties.

You will discover that a single hour of purpose is more powerful than a whole day of confusion. Great lives are built on small completions, not dramatic declarations.

A giant oak does not grow from a forest of seeds, but from the discipline of one seed that stays in the soil. Think of each day as a single seed. If you improve by just 1 percent each day, over a year, this adds up to a remarkable 37-fold increase. This is known as the power of small, consistent improvement. Begin with one task today, complete better than yesterday, and observe how these incremental advances accumulate into significant progress. Imagine saving just 1 percent more, reading 1 percent longer, or exercising 1 percent more intensely each day. Over time, these small improvements compound and magnify, like interest accrued in a savings account, demonstrating the strength of perseverance.

As you strive to approach every day with purpose, don't rush to achieve monumental success. Instead, focus on completions first. Finish that task, complete that project, check off that one box. It's the minor victories that lay the foundation for bigger accomplishments.

Think of it like this: finishing a marathon is great, but it begins with completing each training session, each mile, each quiet run when no one is watching. Completions build discipline, confidence, and momentum.

Once you've mastered the art of finishing what you start, you'll be ready for larger accomplishments. You'll be able to address difficult projects, overcome obstacles, and achieve what formerly appeared impossible.

In the end, the size of the achievement will not matter as much as the discipline and purpose behind it. By focusing on completions, you'll set yourself up for success and create a foundation for accomplishments that will last a lifetime.

Paul once wrote:

"For all things I have the strength through the One who gives me power."
— Philippians 4:13

And another verse adds a resolute yet freeing reminder:

"Jesus replied, 'No one who puts a hand to the plow and looks back is fit for service in the kingdom of God.'" **— Luke 9:62**

Forward. One row at a time. One day at a time.

The Car Mirror Law

Later that afternoon, as Marius walked past a parked car, its windshield caught a blade of sunlight and threw it across his eyes. The glare pulled up a memory - something Cornelius had said in passing, wrapped in one of his simple, unsettling metaphors:

"Life is like driving. You must glance at the rearview mirror - but never stare into it."

Marius hadn't understood then. Now he did.

The past, like the mirror, has its purpose.

It confirms where you've been.

It shows what follows behind.

It teaches what to avoid next time.

But no driver survives by staring at the mirror.

And no soul survives by living in memories.

Some people, Cornelius had said, treat the past like a movie they watch over and over, analyzing, regretting, and replaying it. They miss what lies ahead because they are stuck looking back.

Others refuse to look at the mirror at all - crashing into the same mistakes they refuse to learn from.

Wisdom lives between the two.

A verse he formerly had skimmed suddenly carried more weight:

"Forgetting the things behind and stretching forward to the things ahead…" **— Philippians 3:13, 14.**

Not forgetting, as in erasing, but forgetting as in letting go of the past so it no longer controls the present. Which memory still has a hold on you? Take a time to contemplate this, as it can help you better understand the metaphor.

Cornelius had previously leaned toward him and whispered:

"The past is a teacher, not a destination."

And another line - sharper - stayed with him:

"No man moves forward while gripping what is behind him."

Marius thought of another scripture from childhood:

"No man who has put his hand to a plow and looks at the things behind is well-suited..." **— Luke 9:62**

Cornelius would have explained it:

"You cannot plow a straight line looking over your shoulder."

The past had influenced Marius, yes.

But it could no longer drive him.

He would glance - to learn.

But he would move forward - to live.

And as he made his way home beneath the lengthening traces of late afternoon, he perceived the truth settle in him:

The past is a place of reference, not a place of residence.

Your First Exercise in Present Momentum

That evening, as the city softened into nightfall and the noise of the day merged into a quiet buzz, Marius remembered one of the final things Cornelius had said before they parted:

"Momentum begins in a moment - the smallest one you command."

So tonight, you will begin the same way he did.

Before you go to sleep, when everything is quiet, and your mind is calm, take a single sheet of paper. Not your phone or a digital note. Choose a piece of paper you can feel, maybe with a soft texture. Notice its weight and the quiet sound it makes as you hold it, and let its simple feel ground you.

At the top of the page, write these seven words:

"Tomorrow I will accomplish one thing."

Then pause.

Do not rush to fill the line.

Let the question settle in you:

What one thing - if done tomorrow - would make the day meaningful?

Not what is most urgent.

Not what demands the loudest attention.

Not what others expect of you.

Choose instead what is true, what is needed, what is yours.

For some, it will be a task left undone for months.

For others, a phone call, prolongedly neglected to make.

For some, a stride toward recovery.

For others, a seed toward a new future.

Cornelius explained it this way:

"A day with one purpose is a day with a spine.

A day with a spine can carry a man."

Once you choose it, write it under the sentence, clearly and simply, without apology.

Fold the paper and place it where you will see it first thing in the morning.

Then sleep.

Not with pressure, yet carrying a feeling of direction.

Tomorrow morning, when you rise, do that one thing before all others.

Before the news.

Before the distractions.

Before the roar of the world asks you to live someone else's day.

Complete that single act, however small, and something impressive will awaken inside you:

A subtle power.

A gentle self-belief.

The feeling of your life beginning to move again.

Cornelius once said:

"When a man proves to himself that he can direct one hour, he begins to trust that he can direct a day." Rewrite this line in your own words and place it where you can see it every day, like your refrigerator or your workspace, turning insight into a daily cue. Personal phrasing embeds ownership of the principle. If you practice this routine for just seven days, you will feel the invisible machinery of your life shift. The wheel that once resisted movement will begin to turn. Your mind will stop fighting you and start working with you. However, remember that consistency is a journey, and missing a day is normal. It is not a failure but an opportunity to build resilience and self-compassion. If you find yourself slipping, gently remind yourself of your initial progress and restart without judgment. Each step back can lead to a stronger step forward.

You will rediscover something long forgotten:

You are not powerless.

You are not stuck.

You are not at the mercy of circumstance.

You are capable of shaping your day, and through your day, your destiny.

This simple routine is not a trick, a gimmick, or a motivational slogan.

It is the beginning of your mastery over time.

And mastery always begins with one decisive act.

One choice.

One hour.

One day.

Start tonight.

Your momentum begins with the line you write next.

Closing Words of Chapter One

When the sun finally set on that first day of intention, Marius realized something quietly astonishing: the day had not changed - he had.

He did not win a fortune.

He did not solve every problem.

He did not become a new man overnight.

But he achieved one little achievement, and that changed his outlook. He learned what most people never discover:

A day feels too long only when a man tries to live more than one at a time. But when he sees each moment as a chance to transform, time turns from a burden into an opportunity.

But when he chooses one purpose and gives himself fully to it, the day feels lighter, clearer, and almost manageable, as if time as a concept responds to focus.

Cornelius once told him:

"The man without a purpose repeats the same day for years.

The man who walks with purpose lives new days - days that grow him."

Marius carried that truth into his evening like a lantern.

He had made his day shorter, not by the clock, but by lightening his load.

And as the weight lifted, a delicate hope surfaced, forming inside him, the hope a man feels when he realizes he is not as powerless as he once believed.

Perhaps, he thought, there was a future he might form.

Perhaps the exhaustion that had smothered him for years was not the end of his story.

Perhaps a life could be rebuilt one day at a time, or even one hour at a time.

And now, dear reader, this is where you enter the story. Because somewhere in this chapter, you may have recognized a piece of yourself:

the fatigue of carrying too many tomorrows

the anguish of waking, already overwhelmed

the habit of worrying instead of moving

the long nights of staring at the ceiling, wondering if change is still possible

Invite yourself to reflect each day. Begin to document your journey in a journal. Each evening, take a moment to pen down your 'one thing' and observe how it subtly shifts your path. Reflect on the progress, however slight it may seem. This reflection will not only keep you engaged but also serve as a beacon of your growth over time.

If you saw even a shadow of your reflection in Marius, then his first lesson is already speaking to you:

You do not need to conquer your whole life.

You only need to command one day - this one.

One intention.

One task.

One step.

One tiny win that quietly says, "You can rise again."

Tonight, write your one purpose for tomorrow.

Guard it.

Honor it.

Let it be the beginning of your own present momentum.

Because when a single day is lived deliberately, the mind shifts, the heart steadies, and hope - the quiet kind - begins to return.

And hope is where the next chapter begins.

For beyond the discipline of the present moment lies something deeper, something every struggling soul eventually encounters:

darkness, and the question of whether light can return.

Turn the page when you're ready. Next: Reclaiming Hope in Dark Times.

❧

Chapter Two: Reclaiming Hope in Dark Times

☙

"When the light seems gone, remember: the dawn is not a new sun, but the same one rising again."

— Cornelius.

"We are hard pressed on every way, but not cramped beyond movement; we are perplexed, but not absolutely with no way out."

— 2 Corinthians 4:8, 9

For several days after meeting Cornelius, Marius tried to live as the old man had taught him - not perfectly, not with certainty, but honestly.

He began to shorten his days, not by laziness, but by choosing endings and welcoming quiet.

He learned to command his hours, no longer letting time slip by unnoticed.

He tried to let meaning settle into the places where anxiety used to live.

At first, the changes were small - nearly invisible.

He made his bed each morning. Slowly. Deliberately.

As he smoothed the sheets, it felt as if he were smoothing the disorder in his mind.

Sometimes he walked around the block, greeting the sunrise breeze, letting it cool his face. Other times, he resisted the temptation to drown in the glowing blue gleam of his phone.

The city moved around him, traffic humming, shop doors rolling open, voices climbing and fading, but inside, a calmer force was waking.

Each small action marked a new beginning.

Marius sensed a shift, not in the world, but in himself.

Change didn't shout; it whispered.

It did not arrive like lightning. It arrived like morning: gradual, patient, almost easy to miss.

Many speak of promise as a feeling, a radiance of optimism that appears when things get better. But true hope, Marius was learning, is not a mood.

Hope is a discipline.

It is the quiet decision to move, to speak, to act, even when you do not yet feel the light.

It is not born from circumstances; it is born from courage.

The world frequently mistakes comfort for hope. But comfort is passive; it waits for the storm to pass.

Hope is active; it learns to walk in the rain.

Cornelius had told him once:

"If you can find one thing today that is still worth loving, still worth working for, still worth believing in - you have already reclaimed your light."

Hope is a craft. It must be practiced, shaped, and guarded. It begins when you stop asking life to change and start asking yourself, "What can I bring to this moment that will make it better?"

And slowly, Marius realized: he was beginning to practice the discipline of promise.

The Seed Beneath the Stone

Cornelius once told Marius the story of a farmer who sowed a seed beneath a massive rock.

When the rains came, the farmer worried the seed would never sprout. But when he returned weeks later, he found the stone lifted slightly, shifted by a fragile stem that chose not to die.

"That," said Cornelius, "is what hope does. It lifts what should be unmovable."

The stone represents the burdens of the world - bills, debts, disappointments, hidden wounds, or the loss of a loved one.

The seed represents your determination to begin again, even under pressure.

Even when the soil of your soul feels dry, the seed waits.

It needs only one drop of courage to live.

Cornelius had told him on the bench that first morning:

"You cannot heal a life in a week. But you can reclaim a moment, and sometimes that moment is enough to begin again."

Those words now returned to him like a subtle murmur, steady, similar to a heartbeat.

One evening, sitting at his small kitchen table with a worn cup of tea in his hands, Marius remembered a scripture from his childhood, one he hadn't thought about in years:

"Teach us how to count our days, so that we may gain a heart of wisdom." **— Psalm 90:12**

For the first time, he understood it.

The wisdom was not in counting the years behind him, nor in worrying about the years before him, but in honoring the day he held in his hands.

He remembered mornings at his grandmother's house - sitting with her on the porch, watching the sunrise. Her voice returned:
"Every morning, we get a new chance."

And so, one deliberate breath at a time, Marius began to rise.

The Law of Renewal

Hope does not return the way most people expect.

It does not burst through the door with fanfare.

It does not sweep away all sorrow in a single night.

Hope returns the way morning does - quietly, patiently, line by line across the horizon.

This is the Law of Renewal:

Life will begin to heal itself the moment you permit it.

A single purposeful action, however small, creates light. Even tiny rituals can have a significant impact. Each small step forward, however minor, contributes to the illuminating journey.

One act of meaning becomes one breath of peace.

One breath of peace creates one clear thought.

One clear thought births one decision.

And one decision, faithfully lived, awakens momentum.

Cornelius once placed a hand on Marius's shoulder and said:

"A man in darkness is not broken. He is simply out of rhythm.

And rhythm returns not through emotion, but through motion."

Marius believed him, though he hardly grasped why.

The days ahead still felt unsure, but he noticed something quietly miraculous: even the slightest step toward goodness roused something alive inside him. The world around him began to whisper in colors he had ignored for too long, the rich hues of dusky skies at twilight, the gentle rustle of leaves playing a soft symphony with the wind.

A heightened awareness of life accompanied each awakening: the warmth of sunlight caressing his skin, the earthy scent of rain-soaked pavement, a distant bell chiming in perfect rhythm with his resurfacing hope.

It reminded him of another passage he had heard once but never truly absorbed:

"Do not be anxious about anything..." **— Philippians 4:6**

He had always thought it was impossible - until now.

Perhaps the scripture was not a command, but a beckoning.

An important note that anxiety lives in tomorrow, but strength lives in this moment.

This was the Law of Renewal in its purest form:

The smallest present action is greater than the greatest future worry.

And slowly, quietly, something strongly hidden inside Marius began to breathe again.

When Darkness Becomes Familiar

Despair rarely appears suddenly.

It enters quietly - amid exhaustion, disappointment, and the small betrayals of ordinary life.

Darkness rarely arrives with thunder.

Most of the time, it slips through a side door – gradually - until one day you realize you've lived with it so long it feels like furniture.

It starts when we stop believing our efforts matter. What if someone else's ending is only a trailer, not the full film? When we slip into the trap of comparison, we lose sight of our own journey and diminish the significance of our progress.

It deepens when we compare our beginnings to someone else's ending.

It takes root when we forget that the night was never meant to last.

Cornelius at one time had said:

"Despair is faith inverted."

"It is the belief that tomorrow will be worse than today."

"Hope, then, is simply the decision to believe otherwise."

Marius knew that darkness well.

He had lived with it for years: work noise that never quieted, unpaid bills stacked like accusations, and the slow shame of not becoming the man he once imagined.

It hadn't come all at once - there was no sudden catastrophe, no violent disruption.

Not with catastrophe.

It came through the steady deterioration of confidence, a dream postponed until it blended with surrender.

He lived with darkness the way a man might live with a dim, failing lightbulb; its flicker and fade became normal, making it easy to accept shadows as just another part of the room.

Cornelius had seen the signs the very first day.

It was not the theatrical darkness sung in tragedies or written in poetry. It was the ordinary kind that sneaked into a life through repetition:

the same commute

the same thin paycheck

the same loneliness in packed spaces

the same deadlines that appeared to be like moving targets

the same fear that the following day could look exactly like today

He had lived with that darkness for years before meeting Cornelius.

It wasn't loud.

It wasn't violent.

In time, it became unremarkable - familiar as breathing.

Darkness wins not by force, but by familiarity.

Cornelius once told him:

"The worst darkness is not the kind that blinds you, but the kind you grow accustomed to."

"You've grown used to the dark," he told him later.

"Familiarity is the slyest prison of all."

Marius knew what he meant.

Darkness becomes familiar when:

Fatigue stops being temporary and becomes an identity.

Small failures pile into quiet shame.

The world's noise grows louder than your own inner voice.

You stop believing you deserve a different life.

You confuse survival with living.

He woke each day already braced for disappointment.

He went to work with low expectations.

He returned home, expecting the upcoming worry before it arrived.

He began to believe his dreams were childish, his strength insufficient, his efforts meaningless.

Despair that possessed did not come to him like lightning.

It had built a home in him, brick by brick, thought by thought, hour by hour.

Cornelius understood this and gently dismantled the lie:

"Most men are not defeated by catastrophe, but by the gradual erosion of belief."

He explained that despair is not a sudden fall; it is a slow forgetting.

For a long time, Marius had forgotten what hope felt like.

Forgotten that joy was possible.

Forgotten that purpose kept beating quietly inside him.

And that is why Cornelius said something that first sounded harsh, but later felt like salvation:

"Despair is faith turned inside out.

It is faith in the wrong direction.

It is believing the worst before it happens."

Those words stunned Marius.

He had never thought of misery as a belief, but that was precisely what it was.

Despair says: *Tomorrow will be worse.*

Hope says: *Tomorrow still bears promise.*

Despair peers into the future and sees only loss.

Hope peers into the same future and sees possibility.

Cornelius never forced optimism.

He redirected the lens.

He reminded Marius of a scripture he once skimmed but now understood:

"Stop being anxious about your lives… Observe intently the birds of heaven, … Your heavenly Father feeds them." **— Matthew 6:25, 26**

"Worry," Cornelius explained, "is a story you tell yourself about a future that hasn't happened.

Hope is a different story about the same future."

Then he added quietly:

"You get to choose the story."

For the first time in years, Marius realized that darkness had not chosen him; he had unconsciously chosen to stay inside it.

Not maliciously.

Not intentionally.

But gradually, quietly, through practice.

Hope returned the same way darkness had arrived, not through drama, but through small, deliberate choices:

waking up ten minutes earlier

making his bed with purpose

paying one small bill instead of being afraid of all of them

taking a walk without checking his phone

silencing the noise long enough to hear his own breath

He discovered something astonishing:

Hope does not depend on circumstances.

Hope depends on attention.

Where the mind looks, the heart follows.

Cornelius summarized the lesson with a metaphor so simple that Marius never forgot it:

"The seed planted deepest in your mind is the one your life will grow toward."

Darkness had been his seed for too long.

Now he began planting something else.

One morning, Marius remembered another scripture:

"We are hard-pressed in every way, but not cramped beyond movement… perplexed, but not absolutely with no way out." **— 2 Corinthians 4:8–9**

And Cornelius whispered, as though finishing the verse:

"The night tests you.

The dawn rebuilds you."

Hope did not flood his life at once.

It tiptoed back in.

A breath at a time.

An action at a time.

A day at a time.

Slowly, the darkness loosened its grip.

Slowly, Marius realized that despair possessed no power over a man who refused to surrender the present moment.

Cornelius once said:

"When you cannot see the light, remember it is still shining, even if it must reach you through memory first."

And so, Marius learned something substantial:

Darkness becomes familiar, but hope becomes faithful if a man chooses to rise today.

The Practice of Beginning Again

Every morning, life gives you a blank page disguised as routine. Most people overlook it because it looks ordinary. But to the wise, every morning is a contract renewed between you and time.

If yesterday failed you, rise anyway.
If your plans fell apart, start smaller.
If your heart aches, breathe gently and say, "Still, I am here."

This is courage: not escaping pain, but refusing to surrender to it.

Cornelius once said:

"You may not be able to rewrite the past, but you can still edit the next line."

When the Old Self Resists the New Life

Change, Cornelius said, is the only thing in life that never needs permission. It arrives on its own timetable - quietly, steadily, often inconveniently.

Marius remembered a morning when he was headed to a meeting and missed his bus by seconds.

Frustration welled up, but as he stopped to breathe, he noticed the calm around him - people moving, the sun casting gentle light on the buildings, a bird singing. With the next bus not due for another fifteen minutes, he walked instead, and in that quiet stroll, he realized that change sometimes involves simply accepting the unexpected.

That small moment taught him that while plans may falter, his spirit need not. This lesson imprinted in him the truth that Cornelius often shared: change is woven into life's fabric in ways both grand and ordinary.

But there is another truth he uttered gently to Marius a certain evening as the city's lights shimmered against the café window:

"The hardest battles are never fought against the world."

"They are fighting against the parts of you that fear becoming someone new."

Marius felt that deeply.

Because as he tried to reclaim hope - to rise again, to shorten his days, to choose one meaningful act at a time - something in him resisted.

Not loudly.

Not violently.

But persistently.

It was the old self: the version of him that had survived inside worry and exhaustion. The version that knew how to function in chaos, but not in peace. The version that could endure misery, but did not yet know how to embrace possibility.

Cornelius called this resistance:

"The whisper of the man you used to be."

"Every time you grow," he spoke quietly, "the old version of your panics.

It wants routine.

It wants certainty.

It wants the predictable misery it understands."

The old self whispered:

"Stay where you are. At least you know how to survive here."

"Don't change too fast - you'll only disappoint yourself."

"Why try again? The past will repeat."

Marius was learning something essential:

The familiarity of pain is often more seductive than the uncertainty of healing.

Consider this: *What predictable misery have you grown accustomed to?*
Naming it may be the first step toward leaving it.

"People do not remain stuck because they lack strength," Cornelius said.
"They remain stuck because they fear the price of stepping into the new."

Scripture softly spoke the same truth:

"Do not remember the former things; and do not dwell on the past.

Look! I am doing something new…" **— Isaiah 43:18–19**

Even nature testified:

Seasons do not ask permission to change.

A seed does not negotiate with the soil before breaking open.

A caterpillar does not cling to crawling when its wings begin to form.

But humans - especially wounded ones - resist what would transform them.

Marius resisted, too.

He resisted joy because he feared it would disappear.

He resisted peace because he didn't trust its silence.

He resisted change because the familiar darkness had become his identity.

Cornelius steered him through this resistance with simplicity:

"Your old self is not your enemy.

It is your evidence.

It shows you who you used to be so you can recognize who you are becoming."

Marius learned to treat his resistance with patience.

Each time he stepped into a new discipline - waking early, walking, completing one meaningful task - the old self pulled at him like gravity.

So, Cornelius gave him an analogy that stayed:

"Old habits are like worn shoes.

Comfortable, familiar, and full of holes."

To illustrate, he took Marius to a shoe repair shop where a worn pair sat on a shelf, threadbare and bent.

"People keep shoes like this," the cobbler said, "because their feet know them. But one day they must choose a new pair, not because the old ones were evil, but because they can no longer carry the journey ahead."

Cornelius looked at Marius:

"The life you lived before cannot carry the life you're trying to build now."

Another scripture echoed this law:

"Do not say, 'Why were the former days better than these?' For it is not out of wisdom that you ask this." **— Ecclesiastes 7:10**

The past, no matter how painful or precious, is always limited.

It can teach.

It can guide.

But it cannot lead a man forward.

To move forward, Marius had to do something he never imagined:

He had to let go of the version of himself that had upheld him this far.

He wrote in his notebook:

"Yesterday's strength cannot lift tomorrow's dreams."

Cornelius nodded when he showed him.

"The road ahead demands a stronger, clearer, more deliberate man.

And that man is already within you - waiting for room to grow."

This became the foundation of Marius's renewal:

He learned to welcome discomfort rather than fear it.

He came to accept uncertainty, not avoid it.

He learned to interpret resistance as proof of transformation.

He learned to let go, not out of loss, but out of necessity.

He learned that change is not the enemy; stagnation is.

Paul's words came alive in him:

"One thing is certain: Forgetting the things behind and stretching forward to the things ahead…" **— Philippians 3:13**

With that same gentle bravery, Marius moved forward:

not perfectly,

not quickly,

but faithfully.

One hour at a time.

One habit at a time.

One version of himself at a time.

He discovered that the Law of Change was not there to frighten him, but to free him.

And as he grew, something astonishing happened:

The old self stopped fighting because the new self-started leading.

The First Signs of Light

Darkness does not vanish the moment a man decides to change.

It lingers... It questions... It tests the sincerity of his hope.

"Darkness always checks twice," Cornelius told him once.

"First to see if you are awake, and then to see if you are serious."

Marius felt that truth.

Even after small steps into renewal, there were moments when heaviness returned - softer than before, but familiar enough to tempt him back.

The human heart can grow accustomed to sorrow. Some sadness becomes so familiar that releasing it feels like losing a part of yourself.

Marius felt that pull often, the invitation to slip back into numbness, to return to the mechanical living of yesterday.

However, something had begun to shift -

not loudly,

not dramatically,

although unquestionably.

It began with a single unexpected moment.

One sunset, after finishing a task he had promised himself he would complete, Marius walked outside and noticed something he had not seen in years:

There were stars.

Real ones.

Bright, distant, calmly pulsing amid the calm sky.

He stood there a long while, hands in his pockets, his breath slowing, feeling as though the night alone had finally exhaled.

Cornelius's voice whispered in memory:

"Even the slightest bit of light is enough to declare war on the darkness."

Marius recognized then that change wasn't something he forced into existence.

Change was something he made room for.

And when he made room, light entered - gently, like a guest who knocks and waits to be welcomed.

The first signs of light came in small ways:

He laughed softly at something on the radio - genuinely, for the first time in months.

He slept a whole night without waking in anxiety.

He finished a task without cursing himself along the way.

He hummed while making coffee.

He called an old friend - not because he needed help, but because he had the strength to give.

Tiny things. Overlooked things.

But in a man recovering, hope is a miracle.

"Light returns to a man the moment he chooses to look for it," Cornelius had taught him.

Scripture repeated the same truth:

"Stop being anxious about your life…" **— Matthew 6:25**

Worry narrows the eyes until the world becomes a tunnel.

Hope widens them again.

Another passage reassured his heart:

"Do not be anxious over anything, but in every everything…let your petitions be made known to God… and the peace of God… will guard your hearts."**—Philippians 4:6, 7**

These verses did not deny darkness.

They refused to let darkness command the day.

Slowly, the pieces of his inner world began realigning.

He noticed the smell of morning rain again.

He heard the melody in everyday sounds - the buzz of the refrigerator, the whistle of a kettle, the rhythm of steps on the street.

He remembered moments from childhood when life had felt uncomplicated.

He discovered clarity where there had been noise.

This was the first sign of a reborn life:

Awareness.

"Awareness," Cornelius said, "is the doorway through which light enters the mind."

As awareness returned, something notable occurred:

Marius began to see possibilities again - in his work, in his relationships, in his future, in himself.

He understood a subtle truth:

The most dismal hours do not last.

But the lessons they teach do.

One nightfall, he wrote in his journal:

"Maybe the shadow was not trying to destroy me.

Maybe it was trying to prepare me for the strength I would need when the light shone again."

Cornelius's wisdom echoed:

"When you feel the first signs of light, honor them.

Because the faintest glow at daybreak is still proof that the night has lost its power."

That night, Marius slept peacefully - for the first time in years.

Hope had returned.

Not fully.

Not loudly.

Though unquestionably.

And with that first soft voice of light, his new life had begun.

Why Minor Triumphs Matter More Than Big Ones

The next morning, Marius's routine looked strangely ordinary.

He brushed his teeth.

He boiled water.

He prepared a simple breakfast.

Nothing in the room had changed.

No choir of angels announced his progress.

And yet - something inside him was different.

He had won a battle no one else would ever see.

A private, invisible victory.

The kind that feels too small to celebrate… but quietly rewrites the future.

Cornelius had a name for it:

"The Victory No One Applauds."

"Boy," he told him once on the bench, "life changes at times when they look like nothing at all.

Make the bed.

Pay the small bill.

Take the quiet walk.

Choose the calm thought.

These are the tiny depends on which destiny swings."

At the time, Marius thought he understood.

Now he truly did.

Most people wait for breakthrough moments - grand opportunities, sudden clarity, dramatic transformation.

But the human mind does not change through explosions.

It changes through repetition.

Neural pathways don't form when a man has one big victory.

They form when he has one consistent victory.

Even a small one.

Especially a small one.

Cornelius phrased it like this:

"The mind learns who you are

by watching what you do repeatedly."

Not your dreams.

Not your desires.

Not your promises.

Your repetitions.

And on that morning, Marius repeated something his mind had not seen in years:

He showed up for himself.

That was enough to tilt the axis of his life a single degree, and one degree, carried far enough, changes the entire horizon.

Psychologists call this micro-resilience.

Therapists call it behavioral anchoring.

Scripture spoke of it long before:

"The person faithful in what is least is faithful also in much." **— Luke 16:10**

"Greatness hides inside smallness," Cornelius would say.

"Every giant oak begins as an unnoticed seed."

Marius now understood:

A life doesn't change when a man takes big leaps.

It changes when he takes small, steady strides.

After breakfast, he walked outside.

The air didn't just feel cool - it felt kind.

He looked up at the sky, then at the street, noticing the shape of the clouds, the pattern of footsteps, the far-off murmur of life stirring awake.

Yesterday, everything had felt like pressure.

Today, all seemed like a possibility.

He wasn't "cured."

He wasn't "finished."

But deep inside, something had begun:

Hope in motion.

"Hope seldom returns with trumpets," Cornelius once said.

"It sneaks in through tiny acts of obedience."

Now Marius could feel that truth moving quietly through his day.

Letting Go of the Familiar: The Law of Change

Change does not ask permission.

It moves through a life the way a river shapes a stone - slowly at first, then all at once.

Cornelius once told Marius:

"The greatest trap a man ever falls into is the comfort of what no longer serves him."

That was where Marius had been living, not in visible disaster, yet within the calm familiarity of a life that no longer nourished him.

He wasn't alone in this.

Most people cling to what is familiar even when it hurts them, stalls their growth, and keeps them chained to who they no longer wish to be.

Not because the familiar is truly comfortable, but because it is known.

Cornelius called this The Law of Change and spoke of it bearing the burden of experience:

"Everything changes, my boy.

The only question is whether you rise with the change or cling to what is already disappearing."

Change is woven into everything:

Seasons turn.

Rivers shift.

Cities rise and fall.

Friendships evolve.

Dreams sharpen or fade.

People become who they choose - or who they refuse - to be.

Heraclitus once wrote, "The only constant in life is change."

But long before him, Scripture had softly said:

"For the scene of this world is changing." — 1 Corinthians 7:31

It changes with or without our consent.

Marius had been holding onto many things:

a version of himself that no longer existed

dreams formed by who he used to be, not who he was becoming

routines that numbed him instead of strengthening him

memories he recalled because they were safer than beginning again

We cling to what is familiar because:

It asks nothing new of us.

It spares us from risk.

It keeps us near the past.

It delays the discomfort of growth.

But the tragedy is simple:

You cannot hold onto the familiar and reach for the future at the same time.

Again, Isaiah's words reflected:

"Do not remember the former things. And do not dwell on the past. Look! I am making something new." **— Isaiah 43:18, 19**

"A man cannot walk toward the sunrise while looking over his shoulder," Cornelius said.

The image stayed with Marius.

So did another lesson: the story of the cocoon.

Cornelius told him:

A boy once found a caterpillar struggling inside its cocoon.

Feeling pity, he opened it slightly to help the creature escape.

The caterpillar emerged - weak, trembling - but it never flew.

Its wings had not been allowed to strengthen.

The struggle was the preparation.

The cocoon was the training ground.

The resistance was the miracle.

"Some changes feel like endings," Cornelius murmured quietly, "because you cannot yet see your wings."

Growth, Marius realized, never feels safe.

It happens in the vulnerable space between what we were and what we are becoming.

Accepting The Unfamiliar: Gaining Strength through Uncertainty

The unfamiliar has frightened men since the beginning of time.

Not because it is always dangerous, but because it is unlit.

"Men fear darkness," Cornelius said, "not because monsters live there, but because they cannot see their own feet."

Most people resist change simply because they cannot see the outcome.

The mind wants guarantees, contracts, assurances, something solid to hold before taking the first step.

But life has never worked that way.

The path reveals itself only as you walk.

"Clarity does not precede movement," Cornelius told him.

"Clarity follows movement."

He compared it to walking across a bridge in fog:

If you wait for the fog to clear, you will never move.

If you take one step, you discover a firm plank beneath your foot.

Then another.

And another.

Only then does the fog begin to thin.

This is the way of courage, not the lack of fear, but the willingness to walk even as sight is limited.

Many of Scripture's greatest characters acted under this same law:

Abraham walked into a land he had never seen.

Moses progressed toward a sea that had not yet parted.

Peter stepped out of a boat before the waves grew calm.

None of them moved because the path was certain.

They moved because God was.

"The unknown becomes a friend once your feet touch it," Cornelius summarized.

Before meeting Cornelius, Marius had built his life around control, predictable routines, anticipated results, and tight plans.

But life kept shifting: jobs dissolved, relationships faded, bills rose, dreams stalled. Uncertainty made him feel powerless.

"Uncertainty," Cornelius guided kindly, "is not the lack of power.

It is the arena where power is discovered."

Uncertainty forced him inward - to his courage, his resourcefulness, his unused strength.

It asked questions only he could answer:

Who will you be now?

What will guide you?

What will you trust?

Will you step forward or stand still?

In those questions lies transformation.

When Routine Becomes a Cage

Many people pray for change while clinging to the very routines that bind them.

Cornelius painted a picture:

A bird raised in a cage.

One day, the door is opened.

The sky is free.

The wind is calling.

Life is waiting.

And yet the bird remains still.

Not because it cannot fly, but because the cage is familiar.

"Which is worse?" Cornelius asked Marius.

"The cage that confines you, or the cage you refuse to leave?"

The question struck deeply.

Marius realized he had been sitting in an open cage for years - hoping life would change while he stayed exactly the same.

Cornelius reminded him of Israel in the wilderness.

They prayed for deliverance, yet when freedom came, they desired Egypt again, not because slavery was good, but because it was known.

"Men do not fear bondage," Cornelius whispered.

"They fear beginning again."

The unknown, he explained, carries three quiet gifts:

Possibility: that which you dread

may become what frees you.

Perspective: new angles reveal new strengths.

Provision: what you need often waits beyond what you know.

But these gifts appear only to those who step forward.

"Forget the former things… See, I am doing a new thing." **— Isaiah 43:18, 19**

A man cannot see the "new thing" while gripping the "old thing" with both hands.

One afternoon, as he walked his usual route through the neighborhood, Marius stopped at a crosswalk.

A quiet nudge inside whispered:

"Turn left today, not right."

It was a small thing - insignificant to anyone watching - but it was the first time in years he had done something just because it was unfamiliar.

The road was slightly longer, slightly quieter, somewhat less predictable. But something changed in him.

He felt awakened.

He felt in motion.

He felt the air signaling change, even though the street looked unremarkable.

"The unknown does not become less frightening," Cornelius told him later.

"You simply grow braver."

The wiseman added its own anchor:

"The living know that they will die…

Whatever your hand finds to do, do it with your might." **— Ecclesiastes 9:5, 10**

This did not frighten Marius.

It sobered him.

It reminded him that life is too short to live stuck in routines that suffocate the soul.

Change was no longer a threat.

It was a sign that life still believed in him.

Your Real-Life Activity

Tonight - before you sleep - do this exercise.

It will take less than two minutes, but it will begin rewiring your emotional momentum, just as it did for Marius.

Step 1: Get a sheet of paper.

Write this sentence at the top:

"Tomorrow I will choose one small act of courage."

Not a large act.

Not a dramatic act.

Just one small, honest act.

Step 2: Under it, write ONE thing you will do.

Keep it small:

Send one message you've been avoiding.

Clear one corner of your room

Take a 10-minute walk.

Pay one small bill

Drink water before checking your phone.

Read one hopeful paragraph of a book.

Pray one true prayer.

Forgive one small offense.

Decline one unnecessary obligation.

Write one sentence in a journal.

Step 3: Circle it.

Make it visible to your mind.

Your mind believes what your hand writes.

Step 4: Do it tomorrow. FIRST.

Before the noise.

Before the world.

Before the doubt.

Even if you don't feel like it.

Especially then.

Step 5: Notice the shift.

You will feel something - small, quiet, subtle… but real.

A flash.

A breath.

A slight brightness in your chest.

That is the rhythm of renewal beginning.

That is hope returning.

That is your life turning.

Closing Words of Chapter Two

Darkness does not disappear in a single victory.

But neither does hope die in a single defeat.

Every day of renewal - even the smallest day - weakens the hold of despair and strengthens the quiet muscles of courage.

You now know what Marius discovered:

Hope is not a feeling.

Hope is a rhythm.

A rhythm created one action at a time.

Do not underestimate the strength of small motions.

Small motions rebuild destinies.

And if your darkness has lasted for years, remember this:

Night cannot stop the morning.

It can only delay it.

The dawn is already moving toward you with a speed your eyes cannot yet see.

Shorten your day.

Welcome the light it carries.

And prepare your heart, because the next lesson waits in the very place your battles begin:

The Mastery of Thought: The Mind as Builder and Destroyer.

Your deeper strength begins to take shape there.

Chapter Three: The Mastery of Thought - The Mind as Builder and Destroyer

"The greatest battle ever fought is the one between your ears and your heart; your heart writes the script of your life. Make it a bestseller."

— Cornelius.

"Above all the things that you guard, safeguard your heart, for out of it are the sources of life."

— Proverbs 4:23

The Return of the Old Shadows

Discouragement returned before sunrise.

Gloom returned quietly. Marius awoke with heaviness on his chest, that same voice listing his fears.

For a moment, it scared him.

Had nothing changed?

Had all the effort of the previous days meant nothing?

But then another sound entered his memory - Cornelius's calm, level voice under the aged oak:

"The world outside you, my boy, is only a reflection of the world within you."

At the time, Marius thought it poetic nonsense.

Bills didn't disappear with positive thinking.

Loneliness didn't end with a deep breath.

Life didn't soften just because he whispered affirmations.

But now he understood: thoughts determine reality.

They are architects of experience, shaping each day for better or worse.

Each time he allowed despair to write the script, the day seemed to obey it.

Each time he had the courage to think hopefully, even lightly, something improved - a small favor from a stranger, a lighter step, a clearer breath.

It seemed his inner world shaped everything around him.

What if thoughts shape life, not just react to it?

And with that question, he walked into the greatest classroom of all - the furnace of the mind.

The Furnace of the Mind

Across cultures and philosophies, a man becomes what he continually thinks. This principle, found in both religious and secular traditions, shows the profound impact of our thoughts.

Not occasionally.

Not accidentally.

Continually.

Cornelius explained it on a cold evening, voice as calm as the flame beside them:

"Thought," he said, "is the unseen author of every visible reality."

From the firelight to the city skyline, all began as a thought - imagined, shaped, and believed.

Even Scripture testified to this hidden law:

"And God said, 'Let there be light' - and there was light." — **Genesis 1:3**

Cornelius would smile at that.

"See? Even the Creator began with thought spoken into being. Words are thoughts made visible."

But he also warned Marius that the mind is not neutral ground.

There is a war inside every heart, and it starts with thought.

Jesus Himself said:

"The things that come out of a person's mouth come from the heart, and these defile them." — **Matthew 15:18, 19**

And again:

"For from inside, out of the heart of men, come injurious reasonings...

All these wicked things come from within and defile a man." — **Mark 7:21, 23**

Even Jeremiah, centuries earlier, wrote:

"The heart is more treacherous than anything else…Who can know it?"—**Jeremiah 17:9**

Cornelius would fold his hands and summarize:

"The battlefield is within.

Whatever wins there…wins everywhere."

Thoughts aren't visitors - they're seeds.

They grew into beliefs.

Beliefs grew into habits.

Habits shaped character.

Character-shaped destiny.

Thought becomes belief, belief becomes reality. It all starts with thought.

Everything began in the furnace of the mind - silently molding tomorrow while today was still taking shape.

The Two Seeds

Cornelius once told Marius a parable so simple he almost rejected it, until its truth returned to him again and again.

Two seeds lay beneath the soil.

One said,

"It is too dark. I will wait until the sun finds me."

The other said,

"It is too dark. I must rise until I find the sun."

The first seed rotted.

The second broke through the earth and became a tree.

Cornelius's eyes mellowed as he finished:

"Your thoughts are those seeds.

One grows because one chooses action.

The other dies because it chooses to wait."

The lesson was sharp:

Darkness is not your enemy.

Inaction is.

The Law of Mental Correspondence

The universe answers not your wishes but your dominant internal atmosphere.

Cornelius explained it with the clarity of a mathematician and the compassion of a sage:

"You do not attract what you want.

You attract what you are."

A mind focused on lack sees only lack.

A grateful mind sees opportunity.

A fearful mind sees obstacles.

A purposeful mind sees paths.

Even Jesus described this law:

"Whoever has, more will be given…" **— Matthew 13:12**

To the fearful mind, this seems unfair.

But Cornelius corrected him gently:

"No, Marius.

Life rewards stewardship of thought."

A man rich in gratitude becomes richer in peace.

A man rich in bitterness becomes bankrupt in joy.

The mind interprets everything through the lens it wears.

Cornelius summarized it with elegant simplicity:

"Your outer world is your inner world wearing a coat."

The Window Lesson

One afternoon, Marius found Cornelius polishing an old window.

The glass was scratched, cloudy, fogged by years.

"Why bother cleaning it?" Marius asked. "It will never be perfect."

Cornelius smiled.

"Perhaps not.

But it will still let in more light."

He wiped a small circle, and the room brightened slightly.

"The glass is not your fault," he uttered quietly. "But the cleaning is your duty."

He handed Marius the rag.

The mind is this window: polish it to let life's true light in.

If you do not polish it daily, the world looks darker than it truly is."

Beginning that day, Marius practiced replacing every negative thought:

I am alone → I am growing much stronger and more aware.

I am forgotten → I am preparing for my rise.

I am failing → I am learning how to build.

Small substitutions.

Daily polishings.

Marius polished his mind daily. Light returned each day he chose new thoughts. Now, try your own small substitution and see the change.

The Power of Substitution

During one evening, Marius confessed something heavy:

"I try to stop thinking negatively," he said. "Yet the harder I fight the thoughts, the louder they become."

Cornelius chuckled knowingly.

You've found the mind's law: it's filled by intention, not emptied by force.

He continued:

"The more you say, 'I must not think of failure,' the more your mind paints failure."

Marius blinked. "Then how do I stop?"

"You don't," Cornelius said. "You replace.

The mind is not a battlefield to clear.

It is a garden to tend.

If you do not plant flowers, the weeds return every morning."

He quoted **Philippians 4:8**:

"Whatever things are true… honorable… pure… think on these things."

Not as a command, as a strategy.

Thoughts are squatters.

Vacancy invites occupation.

A filled mind brings peace.

Marius wrote it in his notebook:

"An empty mind is a vacancy sign.

A filled mind is a fortress."

The Thought Factory

Cornelius once described the mind in vivid metaphor:

"Every morning, your thoughts clock in for work.

Some build.

Some break.

Some wander.

Some sabotage."

He tapped Marius's chest.

You are the foreman. Direct your thoughts with purpose.

Assign each thought its task."

Gratitude → morale.

Purpose → direction.

Faith → quality control.

Then Cornelius said something Marius never forgot:

"The mind that thinks in order produces a life of order.

The mind that thinks in confusion produces a life of confusion."

The Mirror of Faith

Faith was not mystical optimism.

It was mental chemistry.

"Faith," Cornelius said, "is the architect that drafts the unseen."

Napoleon Hill called it "the head chemist of the mind."

Jesus called it the measure of manifestation:

"According to your faith, let it be done to you." — **Matthew 9:29**

Marius watched this unfold in his own life.

When he believed he had nothing to offer, people overlooked him. When he believed he could rise again, opportunities found him.

To illustrate this, consider the story of Alex, a recent graduate struggling to find his place in the competitive job market. Initially, Alex saw himself as just another applicant among thousands, which manifested in his interviews as uncertainty and doubt; employers could sense his lack of self-assurance, and he faced repeated rejections.

Inspired by similar principles, he shifted his mindset and began to see himself as a valuable addition to any team. He worked on his skills, confidently highlighted his strengths, and tailored his story to showcase how he could contribute meaningfully. Within a few months, Alex not only secured a job but thrived in his new role, demonstrating that a shift in thought can indeed create a shift in reality.

Faith did not rearrange the universe - like Alex, it rearranged Marius.

And that inner shift changed everything.

Resilience - The Mind's Armor

Resilience is the thought that refuses to surrender.

Cornelius illustrated this through the story of Joseph -

betrayed, enslaved, imprisoned, forgotten.

Yet Joseph protected his inner world.

"Where others saw a prison," Cornelius said,

"Joseph saw preparation."

Pain became refinement.

Injustice became training.

Isolation became elevation.

Years later, Joseph said to the very brothers who betrayed him:

"You meant this for evil, but God meant it for good."

Cornelius whispered:

"That is the sound of a resilient mind, a mind that interprets pain through purpose."

Resilience never denies reality; it redefines it.

The Law of Elasticity

Thought is like tempered steel.

The more it bends under pressure, the stronger its ability to return to shape.

Cornelius said:

"The storm does not come to destroy the tree.

It comes to teach it how deep its roots must go."

What once broke Marius now only bent him.

What once bent him began to shape him.

The Threefold Test of Thought

Cornelius taught him to test every thought:

1. Is it TRUE?

    Or is it fear pretending to be fact?

2. Is it USEFUL?

    Will it push me forward or freeze me?

3. Is it KIND?

Would I say it to someone I love?

Any thought failing this test was dismissed like smoke in the wind.

Exercise: The Daily Mind Cleansing

Each morning before the morning breaks:

1. Gratitude - list three small things.

2. Affirmation - speak one truth aloud.

3. Visualization - see yourself acting on that truth.

4. Rejection - when a negative thought appears, say:

"This does not belong to me."

Over time, the mind obeys discipline like a trained muscle. Begin your mind cleansing practice today and see the improvement for yourself. To track your progress and stay motivated, consider setting aside time each week to journal or reflect on your mindset shifts. This reflection can help you recognize growth, keep you encouraged, and make your journey tangible.

The Parable of the Two Mirrors

In a tailor shop, Cornelius showed Marius two mirrors:

One warped.

One clear.

"Stand before the first," he said, "and you appear twisted.

Stand before the second, and you see truth."

Then he touched Marius's chest.

"These mirrors are your mind.

Fear warps.

Faith clarifies.

You must choose your reflection."

That night, Marius wrote:

"I will polish my mirror daily."

The Law in Action

Mastery of thought does not guarantee perfect thinking.

It guarantees awareness.

It guarantees correction.

It guarantees dominion over the inner world.

Every time Marius substituted fear for faith, resentment for thankfulness, doubt for a decision, his future shifted.

Creation was happening inside him.

Quietly.

Daily.

Faithfully.

Closing Words of Chapter Three

You are not a prisoner of thought.

You are its author.

You are not the reflection of your environment.

You are its interpreter.

Guard your mind.

Shape your thoughts.

Build with intention.

Speak with purpose.

Cornelius once told Marius:

"The world is built twice - first in the mind, then in matter.

The man who builds wisely within never fears what crumbles without."

Remember:

You become what you continually think.

Your thoughts are seeds.

Your mind is soil.

Your future is the harvest.

And now you are ready for the next truth, a truth shaped in the flames of fear and the determination to rise above it. Facing Fears and Overcoming Doubt, the battle every rising soul must fight, is next. In the upcoming chapter, practical tools and actionable strategies will be revealed to help you confront these challenges, building anticipation and ensuring the value of life that lies ahead.

Chapter Four: Facing Fears and Overcoming Doubt

"Courage is not the absence of fear, but the mastery of it."

— Cornelius.

"Be courageous and strong. Do not be struck with terror or fear, for Jehovah your God is with you wherever you go."

— Joshua 1:9

The rain came down steadily that afternoon, that turns the world silver and softening the edges of everything it touches. Marius sat on the floor beside his window, legs crossed, a half-open journal resting on his knees. The sheets were a collection of unfinished attempts - lists, goals, half-born dreams, scribbled declarations like "someday," "maybe next month," and the most honest one of all: "when I'm finally ready."

But ready never came. Not for years.

He ran a finger over the words and perceived a subtle truth press against him like the burden of the rain on the glass:

Fear had been running his life.

And he had been calling it "caution."

A sour ache rose in his chest, not pain, though awareness. He snapped the journal shut, stood, and grabbed his coat. Something inside him - worn, but still alive - urged him out the door.

The air outside was cool. Water grasped the city like breath on a mirror. Yet Marius walked with purpose, letting the rain sting his cheeks, letting the cold sharpen his senses. The park was nearly empty when he arrived. The benches were wet and shiny. The grass bowed under the burden of water. The sky dangled low and metallic.

And there, under the same elm tree where everything began, sat Cornelius -coat gathered around him, hat dripping steadily, posture calm as if he had been expecting Marius all along.

Cornelius turned his head and smiled without surprise.

"You came on a stormy day."

"Most people stay home when it rains."

Marius lowered himself onto the bench beside him.

"I was tired of staying home," he said.

"I was tired of waiting for things to change."

Cornelius's look softened, pleased.

"Then you're ready."

"To learn about fear."

The Nature of Fear

The old man lifted his face toward the cloudy sky.

"Fear is not your enemy.

It is your messenger."

A gust of wind fluttered over the elm above them.

Cornelius drew a line in the wet soil with his cane.

"Every man is born with fear - the child fears the dark, the youth fears failure, the adult fears loss, the old fear death."

He tapped the line gently.

"But the wise learn this:

Fear is unspent courage, raw energy waiting for direction.

It is the fire you have not yet learned to handle."

Marius exhaled slowly, breath joining with the cold air.

"Then how do I master it?"

Cornelius grinned softly.

"You master fear as you master fire.

Not by extinguishing it,

but by learning how to hold it."

He shifted closer, tone lowering.

"Fire can burn your house down…or it can bake your bread.

Fear can paralyze you. Or it can prepare you."

Marius listened, rain dripping from the brim of Cornelius's hat in a gentle beat.

"Fear is neutral," Cornelius said.

"It is your interpretation that makes it destructive."

The Mind's Shadow

They sat in silence for a moment, watching raindrops dart down the railing of the bench.

“Fear begins in the mind,” Cornelius said at last.

“A shadow cast by imagination.”

He pointed at a puddle beside their feet.

The branches above it cast a dark reflection - longer, more distorted, more ominous than the real tree.

“The mind,” Cornelius continued,

“Creates shadows larger than the object that casts them.”

Marius swallowed.

He knew that truth in his bones.

For weeks, he had delayed opening a stack of bank letters, terrified of what they might contain. When he finally opened them, the issues were real, but solvable. Yet, Marius realized that not all fears were as straightforward. Some fears had deep-seated roots, stemming from past experiences or complex personal challenges. This acknowledgment brought him a sense of empathy for others who might face fears of a different kind, where the solutions were not as clear or immediate.

“Every fear shrinks when faced,” Cornelius said.

“Every doubt grows when avoided.”

He rested his cane against the bench.

“Fear is only a shadow.

Face it, and it dissolves."

The Two Josephs: Courage In Stillness

Cornelius leaned back, raindrops pattering out a soft cadence around them.

"You remember Joseph," he said.

"The one who rose from prison to the palace."

Marius nodded.

"Courage," Cornelius continued,

"It is beyond merely endurance.

It is using your gifts even when your future is hidden."

He let the thought pause in the rain before speaking again.

"But there is another Joseph -the carpenter of Nazareth."

Marius turned, interested.

"When Joseph learned Mary was with child," Cornelius said quietly,

"His world must have collapsed.

His reputation, his pride, his future - all in danger."

Marius pictured it. The shock. The confusion. The whispers of neighbors. The soreness of betrayal - or at least the appearance of it.

"Yet Joseph did not react in anger," Cornelius said.

"He paused.

He chose stillness.

He refused to decide while the fire inside him continued to burn."

Cornelius's gaze tightened.

"Most people today file for divorce before they even breathe.

They end friendships in the heat of emotion.

They quit jobs, abandon dreams, walk away from miracles -

because fear shouted louder than wisdom."

He looked at Marius with a penetrating calm.

"Joseph waited long enough to hear from heaven.

His courage was not loud.

His courage was stillness."

Marius experienced a chill unrelated to the rain.

"So sometimes courage is not action."

"Sometimes courage is waiting."

Cornelius nodded.

"The strongest people are often the ones who pause the longest."

He lifted his chin toward the clearing sky.

"When fear rushes you, faith asks you to slow down."

The Law of The Lion

The rain eased. A shaft of pale ray reached through the clouds.

"A lion," Cornelius said,

"Does not enter the forest without fear.

It enters with fear, but it does not stop."

He tapped Marius's chest gently.

"Bravery is not the lack of trembling.

Bravery is faith standing on trembling legs."

Marius felt something move deep within him, a lost strength waking.

"You do not conquer fear by running from it," Cornelius said.

"You conquer fear by walking with it - one step further than the last time."

The Silent Fetters

"Fear," Cornelius said, "does not imprison the body.

It imprisons the future."

Marius lowered his eyes. "Sometimes it feels like fear sits on my chest."

Cornelius examined him closely, but gently.

"That pressure is not fear.

"It is your potential, pressing to be used."

He paused.

"Wherever it hurts to go, there lies your next freedom."

Marius closed his eyes.

That sentence alone was worth the entire storm.

The Furnace of Doubt

"Fear," Cornelius said, "is loud.

Doubt is quiet, and far more dangerous."

Doubt does not shout; it seeps.

It enters like water through hairline cracks:

One unanswered prayer.

One delay.

One rejection.

One silent disappointment.

And soon, the mind - once strong - begins to erode.

Cornelius pointed toward a rock in a small stream nearby.

"That rock looks solid," he said.

"But let water run over it long enough, and it will wear away."

Marius watched the stream swirl around the stone.

"Doubt is erosion," Cornelius said.

"Not an explosion."

"How do I stop it?" Marius asked.

"By standing firm," Cornelius answered. "You cannot stop the water from flowing, but you can refuse to move."

He placed his hand on Marius's shoulder. "At the moment doubt enters the furnace of the mind, do not flee the heat. Endure it - and it will purify you."

Cornelius whispered, "Faith does not begin when fear disappears. Faith begins the moment you walk forward in spite of fear."

To counter doubt, practice speaking affirmations, like: "I am capable of overcoming challenges." Let these words anchor your mind when doubt begins to surface.

He let the pause deepen. "Let doubt whisper behind you, never before you."

"At the moment doubt enters the furnace of the mind, do not flee the heat.

Endure it - and it will purify you."

Cornelius whispered:

"Faith does not begin when fear disappears.

Faith begins the moment you walk forward in spite of fear."

He let the pause deepen.

"Let doubt whisper behind you, never before you."

Marius breathed the words in like oxygen.

"I will stand like the rock," he spoke quietly.

Cornelius nodded.

"Good! Then you are already conquering."

The Parable of the Bridge

Cornelius told him a story:

"Two travelers came upon a broken bridge.

One turned back, saying,

'It cannot be crossed.'

The other moved ahead, saying,

'If it can be built,

I will build it.'

The second man reached the other side -not because the bridge was whole, but because he was."

Cornelius smiled.

"Faith is the courage to lay planks beneath your own feet."

The Discipline of Facing Fear

Cornelius offered a simple, transformative exercise: Name the fear. A fear named is a fear reduced. Trace its origin. Most fears are inherited, not chosen. Measure its cost. Fear always takes more than it gives. Act small. One action in twenty-four hours breaks fear's illusion. For example, if one feels anxious about public speaking, they could start by practicing in front of a mirror or with a friend. This breaks the larger fear into manageable actions. Fear cannot survive in a life where action lives.

The Law of Transmutation

"When fear strikes," Cornelius continued, "It releases enormous energy."

He spread his hands.

"Run - and that energy becomes panic.

Stand - and that energy becomes power.

Act - and that energy becomes momentum."

Cornelius's eyes radiated.

"The man who works while afraid soon learns he was stronger than fear itself."

Faith and Focus: The Twin Anchors

Faith without focus is sentiment. Focus without faith is a strain. Together, they become unshakable. Faith says: "Something good awaits me." Focus says: "I will act as though it already has." United, they leave fear no oxygen.

Consider the story of an athlete training for an upcoming race. His faith whispers to him that he can cross the finish line a winner, envisioning the victory long before it comes to pass. Yet faith alone is not enough; it must be paired with focus. Each day, he hones his skills, meticulously planning his regimen, improving his form, and maintaining an unwavering dedication to his goal. In this tapestry of belief and concentrated effort, the abstract concepts of faith and focus are woven into reality, propelling him resolutely toward success.

The Bridge to Peace

Weeks later, Marius found Cornelius again at dusk. The fountain glowed, and the wind bore jasmine and remote laughter. The world appeared gentler, somehow.

“Do you still feel fear?” Cornelius asked.

“Yes,” Marius said honestly.

“But it no longer rules me. It visits, but it does not stay.”

Cornelius’s eyes shone with quiet pride.

“Then you have learned well. Fear may knock, but you decide who enters.”

“What is courage, really?” Marius asked.

Cornelius answered without hesitation:

“Courage is opening the door to fear, learning what it came to teach you - and then showing it the way out.”

Closing Words of Chapter Four

Fear is not your enemy. It is the hallway. Experiencing setbacks in facing fear is normal; what defines courage is the continual practice of standing up after falling. Doubt is not your failure. It is the threshold. Every step you take toward the light, even trembling, even uncertain, weakens fear’s grip and strengthens the muscles of courage.

Cornelius once said:

“The truly courageous are not those who feel no fear. They are those whose hearts quiver - but whose feet still move.”

That night, as Marius made his way home beneath a clearing sky, the last drops of rain shimmered on the pavement like sprinkled diamonds. He did not rush to escape the storm.

He walked through it.

Because he finally understood:

Storms do not come to stop you.

They come to strengthen the man who will rise after them.

And rising is precisely what the next chapter requires.

Chapter Five: Failure - The Hidden Curriculum of Success

❧

"The man who refuses to rise after falling has not failed; he has surrendered. But the one who stands again, though trembling, has already won."

— Cornelius

"For the righteous one may fall seven times, and he will get up again."

— Proverbs 24:16

The Stillness Following a Fall

Every great soul stops at the cliff where dreams splinter in their hands. In that raw instant - heart pounding, hopes slipping through their fingers - the true key to triumph emerges: failure is not a dead end, but a stinging stepping stone to success.

Plans that once sparkled now collapse into dust.

The applause stops.

The room empties.

So-called friends vanish - "Wealth attracts many friends, but the poor man will be deserted even by his friends" **(Proverbs 19:40).**

There is only silence now - tense and oppressive. Even your own breath against the hush is a thunderclap, each heartbeat echoing in the empty space where hope used to live.

Marius knew that silence.

Weeks had passed since his last real conversation with Cornelius. Marius rebuilt his life through small jobs, slowly restoring his confidence. With each completed task, he felt a gentle power grow within, a renewed sense that he still had value to offer. Hope seemed weak, yet real.

Then, one morning, he opened an email - the proposal he'd quietly staked his last hope on was rejected. His chest tightened as the world shrank around him.

Another door closed, and another promise turned hollow.

Another promise turned hollow.

Another "almost" escaped his grasp.

The old whisper slithered back- a sharp, familiar sting. That cruel, intimate voice hissed, "Why try again? You never get anywhere; you always end here."

He slumped at his small kitchen table, staring at a blank, accusing page. Pen poised, hand trembling. The ink refused to flow. His faith, once brilliant and burning, is now only a faint ember, smothered by thick ashes of disappointment.

The silence pressed in, heavy and close, squeezing the air from the room, until even hope seemed to vanish.

And then, as though pulled to that very silence, Cornelius appeared again.

"Back to staring at the void, are we?" the old man asked calmly, a half-smile softening his features.

Marius exhaled - a shudder, not a sigh. His shoulders sagged, as if the weight of every failure had collapsed onto him at once.

"I don't think I have another start left in me."

Cornelius leaned forward, his eyes calm but piercing.

"My boy," he whispered softly, "every breath is another start. The question is not whether you can begin again - it is whether you dare to."

The Anatomy of Failure

Failure is never fatal until it is accepted as final.

A man's defeat is not written in the fall itself, but in his refusal to rise. Life does not condemn the fallen - it only asks a single question: Will you stand again?

Now, pause briefly to think, what new name would you give to your failures? How could redefining this concept bring about personal growth? Write down your thoughts while you reshape this abstract definition into a concrete exercise that acknowledges failure as a rich soil for rebirth.

Will you stand again?

Every failure takes away illusion.

It reveals who you truly are - not who you pretended to be when things were easy.

"Failure," Cornelius once told Marius, "Is not an ending; it is a mirror that shows you which tools you still need to build your success."

The key is to look into this mirror with an honest eye and consider your own life: where have setbacks highlighted gaps, whether in skills or understanding? Perhaps a failed project at work indicates a need for better communication, or a misunderstanding in a relationship shows the necessity of vulnerability.

Learning to decode these signals can transform temporary defeats into enduring growth.

"Failure is feedback," Cornelius emphasized.

It is life's coded message saying:

Adjust your aim.

Refine your faith.

Strengthen your will.

Step out of your comfort zone.

Change your strategy.

Most people never decode that message.

They read, "You failed," and translate it as, "You are a failure."

But the two are not the same.

The Law of Regeneration

Nature itself insists that beginnings are born from endings. The forest fire roars through the trees, devouring what stands. In the aftermath, the air is permeated with the faint yet unmistakable fragrance of charred earth, combining with the sweet promise of wildflowers beginning to bloom. Yet from the ashes rises new growth, thicker, deeper, richer than before.

The seed must split to sprout.

The night must yield to make room for the dawn.

"Unless a grain of wheat falls into the ground and dies, it remains just one grain; but if it dies, it then bears much fruit." **— John 12:24**

Cornelius called this the Law of Regeneration.

"What feels like death," he said, "is often disguised renewal."

Your old plans and ways may fall - not to be wasted, but to be transformed.

The Story of Joseph's Rise

Cornelius reminded Marius one afternoon, as they walked past a row of shuttered shops:

"When Joseph was summoned from the dungeon to stand before Pharaoh, he was the same man who had been forgotten there - but wiser. The pit had taught him patience; the prison had trained him for purpose. Without those dark rooms, he could not have ruled the palace."

He paused, accepting the weight of that truth sitting between them.

"And so it is with you," Cornelius added softly. "Your disappointments are not detours - they are direction. The place that felt like a burial is often the ground of rebirth."

He looked at Marius with subtle fervor.

"Do not despise your seasons of obscurity," he said. "They are the forges of kings."

The Science of Starting Over

Beginning again is not luck. It is not fate. It is a deliberate formula - the chemistry of renewal. Cornelius discovered this equation through years of reflection and observation. He previously conveyed to Marius a story about how he came across it. After several failed ventures, Cornelius found himself in a small town, where he met a humble artisan who built his life anew after a personal tragedy. The artisan's resilience acted as a wellspring of motivation.

Cornelius wrote it in Marius's notebook one day:

Perception + Decision + Motion = Renewal

Perception: See failure not as punishment, but as instruction. Decision: Choose to rise, not because it is easy, but because it is necessary.

Motion: Take one small action, for movement itself generates faith.

"The soul does not heal by waiting," Cornelius told him. "It heals by working."

When you move - even with nervous hands and an unsure heart - something inside begins to reawaken.

Stagnation feeds shame.

Motion feeds hope.

The Burden of Beginning

Starting again hurts because it demands humility.

You must loosen your grip on who you were to make space for who you can become.

Pride clings to the memory of past success.

Courage reaches for the possibility of another.

Don't forget this…

"Do not remember the former things. And do not dwell on the past." — **Isaiah 43:18**

The courage to begin again is the courage to be small once more - to face misunderstanding, possible ridicule, delicate hope, and the risk of yet another fall.

But remember:

Every great man began small.

And every second beginning often looks smaller than the first - but carries far more power.

Forget who you were in the past; yesterday's chapter is closed.

The fresh start is now.

Take that first tiny step - one step at a time.

It is the start of something greater than yesterday.

"Though your beginning was small, your future would be great."— **Job 8:7**

Marius And the Wall

One early morning, Cornelius led Marius to an old stone wall by the edge of the park. Part of it had collapsed - stones scattered, mortar broken, the structure sagging with time.

"Help me rebuild it," the old man said.

They worked in silence for a while - stacking stones, mixing mortar, setting each rock carefully, their fingers dusted with gray.

"Why rebuild this wall?" Marius finally asked. "It will crumble again someday."

"Perhaps," Cornelius said. "But rebuilding it strengthens me. The wall is not the point - the rebuilder is."

He pressed another stone into place, his hands firm.

"Every time you begin again," he said, "you add a layer of strength invisible to others, but indestructible within. After each stone, I notice a new patience emerging, an endurance deepening, and a skill sharpening. These are the layers that make us truly resilient."

That day, Marius understood something fundamental:

The purpose of starting over is not simply to rebuild what existed - but to transform the one who rebuilds.

The Momentum of Tiny Achievements

To rebuild a life, begin with minor victories.

Clear the desk.

Call the friend.

Write the page.

Take the walk.

Wash the dish.

Send the application.

Do not despise simple tasks - they spark momentum and ignite a fire. This scripture comes up again,

"Who has despised the day of small beginning?" **— Zechariah 4:10**

The seed that cracks the earth is smaller than the eye can see, yet it becomes a forest. Momentum is not about speed - it is about persistence.

"Each small victory rekindles belief," Cornelius said. "And belief is the engine of rebirth."

Each minor deed, faithfully repeated, builds a bridge from who you were to who you are becoming.

The Parable of the Potter

"The potter's wheel is forgiveness in motion. Every spin is another chance to begin again." **— Cornelius.**

The workshop filled the air with the aroma of earth, smoke, and warm dust. A thin stream of sunlight fell through a narrow window, painting a bright circle on the spinning wheel.

Cornelius had brought Marius there after discovering what the younger man had tried to hide:

The bottle had found him again.

So had the cigarettes - their smoke ascending like accusations into the night.

The potter worked silently at his bench, sleeves rolled up, and hands covered with clay. Marius watched as the man shaped a vessel from a spinning lump. The continuous hum of the wheel saturated the air, fusing with the natural aroma of wet clay. Under his fingers, the clay rose beautifully, a proof of skill and patience.

But then, the sound of the pottery wheel's steady whir was interrupted by a soft, dull thud as the vessel wobbled, buckled, and caved inward, sending a small splash of clay onto the ground.

Marius winced. "That's me," he spoke in a calm voice.

Cornelius gave a subtle smile. "Then you're in good company."

The potter didn't curse, didn't fling the ruined clay away.

He pressed it down again, added water, and started again.

Each motion was patient.

Steady.

Forgiving.

"You see," Cornelius murmured, pointing to the wheel, "a true potter never despises what collapses. He doesn't throw the clay away. He wets it, reshapes it, and gives it another turn."

He turned to Marius.

"Do you think God is less patient than a potter?"

The question struck deep.

Cornelius continued, voice composed as the wheel's hum.

"There's a story Jeremiah told - of a potter shaping a vessel that failed in his hands. But instead of throwing it away, he made it again, another vessel, as seemed good to him. That is how life works. Every time we fall, the hands that formed us press again - not to punish, but to restore."

He let the pause fill with the sound of spinning clay.

"You think your relapse proves that you're broken beyond repair," Cornelius said. "But it proves something else - that you're still clay, still moldable, still on the wheel."

Marius gulped nervously, staring at the potter's cracked, sure hands. The clay yielded to every push, every correction, every drop of water.

"I keep failing," he uttered. "I do well for a while, then I give in. It feels worse every time."

Cornelius laid a tender hand on his shoulder.

"The clay that collapses learns humility. The one who fights the wheel shatters. The secret, my boy, is not to stay unbroken - it's to stay on the wheel."

He glanced at the brightening window.

"The Potter never quits," Cornelius uttered quietly. "He only waits for the clay to soften again."

That night, Marius walked home with the smell of moist clay still on his hands. He softly spoke into the dark street:

"I am still on the wheel."

He did not stop drinking overnight.

He did not conquer his cravings in a week.

But a change occurred inside:

He stopped calling himself hopeless.

Every morning became not another failure waiting to happen, but another turn of the wheel.

If You Have Fallen

If you are reading this and fighting your own battle - if you've relapsed, broken your promise, or returned to what you swore you'd never touch again - listen closely:

You are not finished.

You are not powerless.

You are not hopeless.

You are struggling - and it is hard. But one stumble does not erase the ground you've already gained. One fall does not define your journey.

You've made it this far. That alone is proof of strength.

Every new day gives you a chance to begin again.

One more choice.

One more "no" to what breaks you.

One more "yes" to the life you're trying to build.

You do not overcome by willpower alone. You overcome by leaning into a strength beyond yourself - the same hands that molded you once are still shaping you now.

So ask yourself:

What makes you vulnerable?

A certain time of day?

A specific place?

A memory?

A particular loneliness or stress?

Identify it.

Prepare for it.

Rehearse, in your mind, how you will face it before it arrives.

Remember Joseph in Potiphar's house - when temptation came, he did not wait to negotiate with it. He refused, and he fled. The strong man does not stand still to test his limits; he moves toward purpose before weakness has time to argue.

You are not alone in this struggle. You have help. You have a choice.

You can choose not to act on destructive desire.

You can accept responsibility for your decisions without drowning in shame for your humanity.

Cornelius once said:

"The potter's wheel is forgiveness in motion. Every spin is another chance to begin again."

So take these steps - simple, but powerful:

Be honest with yourself about your weaknesses.

Identify your triggers and prepare for them.

Choose not to act on the impulses that betray your purpose.

Take responsibility for your choices, not shame for your existence.

Keep testing, learning, adjusting.

You can do this.

You are stronger than you think.

"For all things I have the strength through the One who gives me power."**— Philippians 4:13**

And when you fall again - because some days you will - rise again.

The Potter's wheel has not stopped.

Every turn brings a new shape, a new strength, a new reason to keep believing.

You are not being broken.

You are being remade.

The Courage Equation

Cornelius once wrote a simple formula in Marius's journal:

Fear + Motion + Faith = Courage

Encouragingly, Cornelius explained, “Courage is not the lack of fear, but the mastery of it. The decision to move while afraid, to act before the heart fully agrees, and to speak faith before any proof has appeared.”

To truly understand this equation, try using it as an experiment for a week. Notice how applying Fear + Motion + Faith in small daily challenges can develop your inner strength. Record your thoughts and learnings, noting the shifts in your fortitude.

As Cornelius often said, practice cements courage more effectively than instruction alone.

“Be courageous and strong. Do not be struck with terror or fear.” — **Joshua 1:9**

Every man feels fear.

The difference lies in what he does next.

When you act with fortitude, unseen allies awaken to meet you:

Strength

Grace

Favor

They do not arrive before motion.

They rise to greet it.

The Flame Inside

There is a fire inside every human being that no storm can permanently extinguish.

It may dim, flicker, or hide beneath the ashes of old disappointments - but it does not die.

Your task is to blow gently on that ember until it glows again.

"Let your light shine before men…" **— Matthew 5:16**

Each time you begin again, you breathe life into that flame.

And when it burns anew, it casts light not only for you, but for others who are still stumbling in the dark.

"Courage," Cornelius told him, "Is contagious. To rise is to permit others to rise."

The Ladder of Renewal

Cornelius described renewal as a ladder every man must climb:

Acceptance: Acknowledge the fall without hiding it or self-punishing.

Awareness: Learn what the failure revealed about you.

Adjustment: Change the pattern that led you there.

Action: Move again, even if the step is small and shaky.

Ascension: Let your new wisdom lift you higher than before.

As you rise, consider how your journey might one day guide others as Cornelius now guides those around him. Reflect on the legacy you are building through your steadfastness and the influence you might have as a mentor to those who follow.

"Climb these rungs daily," he said, "and failure becomes fuel."

Marius's New Vision

One morning, when the morning broke quietly, the sky was pale gold, and Marius faced his mirror.

He studied the lines of his face - not as an indictment, but as a record of survival.

"I have lost much," he uttered under his breath, "but I am not lost."

He took his notebook, flipped to a fresh page, and wrote three words in bold, deliberate ink:

Begin Again Today.

It became his private motto.

Every defeat became an instruction.

Each pain is a teacher.

Each closed door is a redirection.

Months later, he found himself leading a small team at a local charity - helping men and women who, like him, believed their lives were already over.

In their eyes, he saw his own reflection:

Broken once.

Burning again.

The Divine Pattern of Renewal

Cornelius watched Marius from a distance one afternoon as the younger man carried boxes, laughed with volunteers, and paid close attention to someone else's story of failure.

Under his breath, the old man softly spoke words that Marius could not hear:

"The God who wrote Joseph's story has not forgotten to write yours."

The author of life specializes in sequels.

He rewrites endings into beginnings,

tombs into wombs,

failures into foundations.

As long as breath remains, the pen is still moving.

Exercise: The Ritual of Re-Beginnings

Each time you face failure - whether public or private - perform this simple deed of spiritual defiance:

Stand up.

Rise physically from the chair, the bed, the ground, the place of defeat.

Speak aloud:

"I am still here."

Recall one past victory.

Remind your mind that it has conquered before.

Take one deliberate action within five minutes.

Call. Write. Walk. Clean. Apply. Pray. Begin.

End the day by writing:

"I have begun again."

With the ink still fresh on the page, take a moment to name one specific action for tomorrow that will move you forward.

This could be a small task, a decision you've delayed, or a move toward a larger goal. By accepting your next action, you create a bridge from reflection to behavior, a tiny commitment that embarks you on another day's journey.

Do this until your subconscious learns the truth:

Nothing can stop you except your own consent.

Closing Words of Chapter Five

Courage is not the roar of the lion.

Cornelius once called it "the whisper of the wounded man who says, 'Tomorrow, I'll try again.'"

The world belongs to those who refuse to stay down.

Joseph rose.

Marius rose.

And you - bruised, weary, uncertain - can rise too.

"Do not dwell on the past. Look! I am doing something new." **— Isaiah 43:18, 19**

Take this truth with you:

You have never truly failed until you stop beginning.

"The greatest act of faith," Cornelius said one winter night, "is not believing you can succeed - it is believing you can start again."

And as Marius walked home through the quiet streets that evening, droplets from a passing drizzle still shining on the pavement, he did not rush from the storm.

He walked with it.

Because now he understood:

The real danger was never in the fall; it was in the rocking chair of worry that keeps a man from ever standing again.

And that, dear reader, is where we must go next.

The Futility of Worry - The Rocking Chair That Never Moves awaits you, where you will learn why anxiety exhausts but never advances, and how to finally step out of the chair and back into your life.

Chapter Six: The Futility of Worry - The Rocking Chair That Never Moves

"Worry is faith in reverse. It creates the very thing it fears."

— Cornelius.

"Who of you, by being anxious, can add one cubit to his life span?"

— Matthew 6:27

The Great Thief of Power

A sharp, chilling gust rattled the city that autumn morning, its whistle threading through cracks and crevices like a spectral lullaby. Marius lay sleepless, trapped in a tremor of visions that danced behind his closed eyes. By sunrise, exhaustion had hollowed him out, leaving nothing but the stark memory of pervasive, restless thoughts.

He walked through the streets with his shoulders bowed, the heaviness of an invisible pressure pressing into him. Every footstep resounded the questions that had tormented him:

What if I fail again?

What if I make the wrong decision?

What if everything I built collapses?

It was not the first time worry found him. Yet, at this moment, he realized its subtle, deceptive nature.

Worry never arrives in thunder.

It seeps in like fog.

It steals slowly, drop by drop, breath by breath.

Cornelius formerly had said:

"Worry is the only tax you pay on a debt you do not owe."

Marius finally understood.

Worry hadn't solved a single problem; it only fed his doubts and drained his strength.

All it had done was siphon his strength for today.

The Parable of the Rocking Chair

When Marius reached the porch, Cornelius was already there, seated calmly despite the cold dampness. A wooden rocking chair groaned below him, its slow rhythm in sharp contrast to the restless agitation within Marius.

"You didn't sleep," Cornelius said without turning.

"No," Marius admitted. "I kept thinking…what if everything falls apart again?"

Cornelius tapped the empty chair beside him.

"Sit."

Marius obeyed.

Confused, Marius gripped the armrests of the chair. He paused for a moment, noticing the cool wood beneath his fingers and the gentle rise and fall of his own breath. Then he pushed.

The chair groaned.

The boards beneath them vibrated.

He rocked back and forth, harder and louder, until breathless, he stopped.

After several minutes, breathless, he stopped.

"Look around," Cornelius said quietly.

Marius gazed across the yard.

The road was unchanged.

The trees stayed unmoving.

Not a single thing had moved, not even him.

Cornelius gave a small smile.

"That, my boy, is worry. Tremendous effort. Zero progress."

Worry vs. Thinking

Cornelius leaned forward, raindrops sliding from the brim of his hat. "There is thinking," he said, and there is worrying. They are not the same."

"Thinking is intention. It gathers facts. It seeks solutions. It moves the mind toward action. Thinking solves problems. Worry is imagination corrupted. It loops. It exaggerates. It stalls. Worry stalls progress. Faith, on the other hand, moves obstacles. Ships, cures, inventions - none were birthed by the anxious. Progress belongs to the calm mind, not the chaotic one."

Thinking is intention.

It gathers facts.

It looks for answers.

It moves the mind toward action.

Worry is imagination corrupted.

It loops.

It exaggerates.

It stalls.

Thinking builds bridges.

Worry circles the riverbank.

Ships, cures, inventions - none were birthed by the anxious.

Progress belongs to the calm mind, not the chaotic one.

The Nature of Worry

Marius stared at the rain collecting beneath the steps. He drew a long breath, feeling the cool air expand his lungs, before exhaling slowly to release the tension coiling within him.

"It feels responsible to worry," he said.

Cornelius shook his head.

"No. Worry only masquerades as responsibility. It is preparation without action, imagination without purpose, fear pretending to protect."

He quoted softly:

"Do not be anxious about anything…" **— Philippians 4:6**

"Notice something?" he added. "The scripture doesn't tell you to ignore problems. It tells you to transfer them - from your mind to God, from fear to motion."

Faith and worry cannot share the same room. One suffocates the other.

The Chemistry of the Mind

When you worry," Cornelius said, "your brain floods with panic."

Marius had once experienced this vividly during a key presentation. As he stood before his peers, his mind went blank, overwhelmed by cascading waves of dread. He stumbled through the rest, barely coherent, haunted by the terror of that moment.

"Vision narrows. Creativity shuts down. Courage thins." The mind built for innovation is hijacked by survival." He placed a light hand on Marius's shoulder. "You cannot think clearly while drowning. Breathe first - then solve."

Worry tightens.

Faith loosens.

Peace begins where control ends.

The Law of Emotional Substitution

"The mind," Cornelius said, "cannot hold two opposite states at once. You cannot inhale gratitude and despair in the same breath."

So, the remedy is not to fight worry but to replace it.

Name one present good, choose the next step, and speak the truth.

In that moment, the inner chemistry shifts.

Fear loses its throne.

"This is not mine to fear. This is mine to learn."

At that instant, the inner chemistry shifts.

Fear loses its throne.

The Storm and the Sparrow

Rain thickened. Cornelius pointed to a sparrow clinging to an elm branch bent by the wind.

"Why doesn't it fly away?" Marius asked.

"Because," Cornelius said, "it knows the storm will tire before its wings do."

He added:

"Observe the birds of the heaven… Are you not worth more than they?"
- Matthew 6:26

Worry is forgetting you, too, have wings.

Faith is remembering the times those wings carried you safely before.

The Futility of Fearful Imagination

Marius confessed, "I imagine every possible disaster."

Cornelius acknowledged with a knowing glance.

"Most men rehearse tragedy instead of possibility. They weaponize their imagination against themselves."

He quoted Job:

"What I have dreaded has come upon me; and what I have feared has befallen me." **—Job 3:25**

"Not superstition," Cornelius said. "Psychology.

The mind magnifies what it meditates on."

Then he moved nearer.

"Change the image, Marius…and you change the outcome."

Cornelius's Anti-Worry Code

"Let's put this into practice, Marius," Cornelius suggested with a reassuring tone. "Start by defining your fear. Speak it aloud."

Marius hesitated for a moment, then said, "I fear my project will fail and I'll disappoint everyone who depends on me."

"Good," Cornelius nodded. "Now, identify what you can control in this situation. What steps can you take?"

Marius thought carefully. "I can prepare thoroughly and seek advice from someone experienced," he responded.

"Exactly," Cornelius encouraged. "Now act immediately on this realization. What can you do right now?"

"I can make a list of potential advisors and set up meetings," Marius decided, pulling out a notebook and beginning to write.

"And finally," Cornelius concluded, "release what remains. Entrust it to time, grace, or God."

Marius closed his eyes, took a deep breath, and whispered, "I release the outcome and focus on my efforts."

"Your energy," Cornelius said, "must go where it helps, not where it drains."

The Shadow Test

At sunset, Cornelius had Marius stand in front of his shadow. The warmth of the late sun cast golden hues over the landscape, painting long, amber shadows on the ground.

"Walk toward it," he said, as the scents of evening magnolia thickened in the cooling air.

The shadow shrank.

"Walk away."

The shadow grew long and distorted, extending like the reaching fingers of dusk. "Fear is like that," Cornelius said. "Face it, and it retreats. Run from it, and it chases you."

The Discipline of Faithful Focus

Focus is the steering wheel of the soul.

Whatever you attend to expands.

Dwell on danger, and fear grows.

Dwell on purpose, and peace strengthens.

Marius dedicated each morning to purpose - writing, studying, planning. During this hour, no interruptions occurred.

Worry found no foothold when his mind was filled with intentional purpose instead.

The Myth of Control

"The worrier," Cornelius said, "builds walls, not windows."

He desires thicker defenses, tighter grips, more guarantees, never realizing that the fortress he builds becomes the prison he lives in.

"The only control you truly possess," Cornelius said, "is over the direction of your next thought."

Joseph couldn't control Pharaoh, only his own reaction. That response opened the gates.

Substitution Through Service

"For sleepless nights," Cornelius said, "there is a cure few men use."

"When your mind circles your own pain, turn the circle outward.

Bless someone."

Send a message.

Make a call.

Offer a prayer.

Give something small.

Worry and self-sacrifice cannot coexist.

One pushes the other out.

"Whoever refreshes others will himself be refreshed." **— Proverbs 11:25**

Even modern science agrees.

The Two Kinds of Problems

"One day," Cornelius said, "you must learn this truth:

There are only two kinds of problems."

Those you can solve.

And those you cannot.

If it can be solved - solve it.

Gather facts. Seek counsel. Think with purpose.

If it cannot be solved, accept it.

Some storms are meant to be endured, not conquered.

"The wise man," Cornelius said, "does not curse the wind; he trims the sail."

Half of anxiety dies the moment you choose which category your problem belongs to.

The Exercise of the Rocking Chair

Marius eventually placed an old rocker in his study.

Whenever he felt the spiral begin, he would sit, rock once, and ask:

"Am I moving - or merely moving in place?"

Awareness returned.

Then clarity.

Then the choice.

The Peace Equation

Cornelius wrote it in Marius's notebook:

Faith + Action = Peace

Fear + Inaction = Worry

Both consume energy.

Only one leads to real progress.

The Still Mind

As the evening fell, Marius found Cornelius in complete stillness beneath the dusk's glow.

"What are you doing?" he asked.

"Listening," Cornelius whispered.

"To what?"

"The calmness separating my fears. It is there that wisdom speaks."

Then he quoted:

"Your strength will be in keeping calm and showing trust." **— Isaiah 30:15**

Stillness is not emptiness.

Stillness is clarity.

The Ladder Out of Anxiety

Cornelius taught him a simple ladder:

1. Pause.
2. Name the fear.
3. Ask what one action is possible now.
4. Do it.
5. Release the rest to grace.

And step by step, the tide receded.

Closing Words of Chapter Six

Worry changes nothing - it keeps you stuck. Only belief and motion create change. Faith changes everything.

You cannot stop every tide, but you can choose the ones you ride. You cannot silence every storm, but you can quiet your soul within it.

"I leave you peace; I give you my peace," Jesus said, "Do not let your hearts be troubled, nor let them shrink out of fear" **— John 14:27**

And as Cornelius told Marius that rainy morning: "A rocking chair moves much and achieves nothing. But a mind anchored in faith can move mountains."

For the coming week, I invite you to place an imaginary rocking chair in your mind. Each time you find yourself worrying, imagine sitting in the chair, asking if you are moving towards a solution or merely swaying in place. Turn that pause into purposeful action, transforming insights into lived change.

The next lesson awaited Marius - a lesson on the force that steadies a man in storms and guides him when the road bends out of sight.

Now, the true journey - discovering the reason for rising - was only starting.

Finding Purpose and Meaning - The Compass of a Renewed Life was already drawing near.

Chapter Seven: Finding Purpose and Meaning - The Compass of a Renewed Life

❧

"A man without purpose is like a ship without a compass - always moving, but never arriving."

— Cornelius.

"For the one who doubts is like a wave of the sea driven by the wind and blown about…the man should expect to receive anything, he is an indecisive man."

— James 1:6, 7

The Gentle Pain of An Unlived Life

Marius had rebuilt enough of his life to function again.

He worked.

He spoke.

He even smiled now and then.

Yet underneath the surface of his days - beneath the routines, the improvements, the careful rebuilding - something deeper stirred.

A quiet longing, an unspoken need.

A question he hadn't voiced: "What is this all for?" The thought brought stillness and self-reflection. Amid routines, deeper meaning is quietly sought. Allowing this question to lead to honest introspection can reveal a new direction.

In the evening, he and Cornelius walked along the riverbank. The sun sagged low behind the city skyline, leaving lines of gold across the water. The river moved steadily, unhurried by the concerns of men.

"I'm surviving now," Marius said. "But I feel like I'm waiting for life to begin. As if I'm walking in circles - going somewhere, but nowhere meaningful."

Cornelius gave a slow nod, neither surprised nor alarmed.

"You are not alone, my boy. Most men stand on that brink. They work hard, they keep moving, but deep down…their life feels like a room they've never fully entered."

He bent to pick up a stone and tossed it into the river. Ripples spread outward - gentle, widening, unhurried.

"See that ripple? It began with a small action. Purpose begins the same way - not with clarity, but with movement."

Marius stared at the widening rings.

"But what if I don't know what I'm meant to do?"

Cornelius offered a subtle smile.

"Then do the next thing before you, and do it with meaning. Identify one small action, no matter how simple, that aligns with your deeper aspirations and decide to pursue it today. Even small steps taken with intent can lead to significant momentum. The one who waits for perfect conditions will wait until life passes him by."

He quoted softly:

"The one who watches the wind will not sow, and the one who looks at the clouds will not reap." **— Ecclesiastes 11:4**

"Waiting for perfect weather," Cornelius added, "is the occupation of dreamers. Living with purpose is the calling of doers."

The Search for Meaning That Never Ends

They walked in silence awhile before Cornelius added something Marius had never heard him say before.

"You know, Marius…the question you're asking, what is the meaning of life? - It's as old as time."

He paused, letting the river breeze brush their faces.

"Men have sought purpose in wealth, in power, in applause, in achievement. They have built towers, chased fame, filled storehouses, and conquered kingdoms. And yet…"

Cornelius looked out across the sparkling water.

"…history is full of wealthy men who felt poor, powerful men who felt weak, successful men who felt empty."

He quoted scripture softly, almost as a subtle tone:

"He opens His hand and satisfies the desire of every living thing." — **Psalm 145:16**

"Why?" Marius asked.

"Because," Cornelius spoke calmly, "material things can fill your hands, your house, your schedule… but they cannot fill your spirit."

He looked at Marius with softness and gravity.

You are not just muscle and memory. You are designed with intention. Like a gardener's hands or a steady pulse, your purpose is connected to your source. Without the Creator, purpose remains elusive. Even those who doubt seek connection - in silence, charity, or science.

The Compass Within

Cornelius crouched and drew a small compass in the dirt with his walking stick.

"Every compass points north," he said, "but it does not walk the traveler's steps for him."

Purpose, he explained, was not a job or title. It was not a measurable achievement. Purpose is direction.

Purpose is direction.

A north for the soul.

"When a man lives without purpose," Cornelius said, "every detour feels like a disaster. Every delay feels like failure. Every hardship feels like punishment." Marius felt a familiar weight in his chest, a gnawing worry about his own aimless path. Was he endlessly wandering through life without any true destination? Doubt crept into his thoughts, questioning whether he'd ever find his direction. But then Cornelius continued, "But when a man knows his direction - even if he walks slowly - he moves with confidence."

Marius followed the outline of the little compass with his eyes.

"So my problem isn't my path," he uttered softly. "It's my direction."

"Exactly," said Cornelius. "The man who knows why he walks will outlast the man who only knows where he walks."

The Noise That Drowns Purpose

They sat on a bench overlooking the river. A bunch of youths laughed nearby. Cars murmured along the bridge overhead. The world flowed, shouted, demanded.

Cornelius sighed.

"Modern life is louder than ever. Screens glow. Opinions shout. Advertisements command. Everyone tells you what you should want, how you should live, who you should be."

"Sometimes," Marius admitted, "I can't tell if the dreams I have are mine, or just echoes from the world around me."

Cornelius nodded.

"You cannot find your direction by following a crowd that does not know where it's going."

Purpose is not loud. It is a persistent, quiet call.

It rises in the still moments when a man turns down the world long enough to hear his own soul.

"In silence," Cornelius said, "a man discovers he doesn't want applause - he wants peace. He doesn't want recognition - he wants meaning. He doesn't want more - he wants what matters."

The Law of Alignment

Cornelius drew three lines in the dirt.

"Life moves with alignment - when thoughts, words, and actions unite in one direction. Where do your lines misalign today? Consider this for introspection."

He tapped each line.

"Thought.

Word.

Action."

"When these moves are together, you create momentum. When they move against each other, you create misery."

A man can dream of greatness but act in fear.

He can pray for peace but speak in anger.

He can desire change but repeat old habits.

"Purpose," Cornelius said, "is when the head and the heart finally shake hands."

He quoted from Paul:

"I am pressing on toward the goal for the prize of the upward calling…"
— Philippians 3:14

Purpose is not discovered in idleness.

It is pursued in alignment.

The Story of Clara: The Woman Who Waited Too Long

Marius once met a woman at a community event - Clara.

She smiled freely but quickly hid her smile, as though joy embarrassed her. She mentioned she used to paint. Her eyes lit briefly, then faded again.

"I stopped," she said. "Life happened. Bills, children, exhaustion. One day I put the brush down… and somehow, years passed."

She looked away.

"I'm waiting for the right moment. The perfect return. When life settles."

Marius remembered **Ecclesiastes 11:4 —** "The one who watches the wind will not sow."

"If you keep waiting," he told her softly, "you may forget how to hold the brush."

Something broke inside her - softly, quietly.

Weeks later, she painted one canvas.

Then another.

Then another.

She sold none of them, yet every brushstroke returned vitality to her face. As Clara stood before the canvas, the faint, earthy smell of oil paint whispered of past dreams and present awakenings. Vivid blues and deep reds mixed under her fingers; colors smeared with intention and emotion.

Each stroke became both a memory and a promise, reigniting her spirit. "I thought purpose was a career," she told Marius. "But purpose feels more like...becoming myself again."

Cornelius later told him:

"Purpose is not measured by applause, but by aliveness."

The Two Journeys Every Soul Must Travel

Cornelius explained one cold morning:

"There are two journeys, Marius, always two."

He held up two fingers.

"The outer journey - work, achievement, survival. And the inner journey - meaning, faith, identity."

Most men succeed in the first and starve in the second. Outer triumph feeds the wallet; inner famine starves the spirit.

When the inner journey aligns, even small outer steps feel sacred.

"When a man's steps match his spirit," Cornelius said, "every road feels like home."

The Storm and The Seed

Late autumn. The sky is brooding. Clouds heavy as wet wool.

Cornelius brought Marius to a field where farmers sowed grain in a coming storm.

Wind shoved their coats. Rain kissed their faces. Still, they sowed.

"They don't wait for perfect skies," Cornelius said. "They trust the soil more than the storm."

He quoted again, his favorite scripture:

"The one who watches the wind will not sow, and the one who looks at the clouds will not reap." **— Ecclesiastes 11:4**

"So, the secret," Marius whispered," is to act even when you're afraid." He closed his eyes for a moment, tuning into the present. He felt the rise and fall of his breath, the gentle assurance of life continuing. In that awareness, the fear did not vanish, but it softened, yielding space for his resolve to grow. "Especially then," he told himself, "When fear reaches its peak, take notice of your breath. Let it steady you as you step forward."

"Especially then," Cornelius replied. "Purpose is born when faith refuses to wait for permission."

The Mirror of The Maker - Why Purpose Is Spiritual

Cornelius spoke with unusual gravity.

"Purpose is not invented - it is remembered."

He looked directly into Marius's eyes.

"You were created, Marius. And creation implies intention."

He recited softly:

"Know that Jehovah is God. He made us, and we belong to Him." **— Psalm 100:3**

"You were not made merely to breathe, eat, work, and die. You were made to reflect the One who made you."

He drew a circle in the dirt.

Inside you is a spark - a reflection of the Creator's own nature. He breathed in.

That is why you ache when you live without purpose. It is not hunger for accomplishment. It is a hunger for alignment.

He continued:

"According to Revelation 4:11, God created all things, and by His will they exist and were created."

"So," Marius said thoughtfully, "purpose begins with the One who designed me."

"Exactly."

"And meaning?" Marius asked.

"Meaning," Cornelius said, "is found in friendship with God."

He quoted again: "Draw close to God, and He will draw close to you." — **James 4:8**

Purpose is far from being simply assignments. But aligning with your Creator.

"God wants to satisfy your desire for meaning," Cornelius said. "It is why He placed that desire inside you."

Modern Miracles of Purpose

Cornelius loved pointing to real lives.

There was Daniel, jobless in middle age, who found his purpose teaching teenagers who had strayed from their path.

There was Anita, who turned her grief for her mother into a support foundation that helped hundreds.

There was Jacob, who began visiting prisons to teach, discovering compassion he never knew he had.

None of them waited for perfect conditions.

They moved forward during storms.

"Purpose," Cornelius said, "is rarely revealed in comfort. It is born in motion."

Purpose Alignment Practice

Cornelius taught Marius a simple exercise. Remembering his own restlessness, Marius engaged deeply with each step:

Step 1: List three things that bring you deep peace when you do them.

Step 2: List three needs in the world that stir your compassion.

Step 3: List three abilities that come naturally to you.

Where these overlap - peace + compassion + ability - lies the seed of your purpose.

"Purpose," Cornelius said, "is where your joy meets the world's need."

Marius practiced this daily.

Some days he failed.

Other days, he flourished.

But he was moving - not perfectly, but purposefully.

The Compass of a Renewed Life

Purpose, like a compass, does not stop storms.

It prevents you from losing yourself within them.

"You may wander," Cornelius said. "You may stumble. You may get lost. But when your compass points true, the path will find you again."

Marius breathed deeply.

For the first time in years, he felt something he couldn't precisely name.

Not certainty.

Not clarity.

Direction.

"Trust the soil," Cornelius whispered.

"Trust the sun."

"Trust the One who gives both."

Marius closed his eyes.

He had found his north again.

Closing Words of Chapter Seven

Purpose is not a final stop - it is a direction.

It is the courage to sow in stormy weather.

It is the decision to walk without guarantees.

It is the belief that meaning will meet you on the road.

He who walks in purpose walks in peace.

He who waits for perfect weather may never begin.

Cornelius's final words that evening persisted like quiet thunder:

"When a man finds his purpose, even his failures become sacred."

And so, Marius walked home beneath the quiet sky - not quickly, not boldly, but with a calm certainty that he was no longer drifting.

Because purpose does not remove hardship, but it strengthens the man who must walk through it.

Ahead of him waited the next great lesson:

The Strength of Resilience: Standing When the World Breaks You.

Chapter Eight: The Strength of Resilience: Standing When the World Breaks You

"When everything is taken from you, what remains is what cannot be taken."

— Cornelius

"Though He may slay me, I would still wait."

— Job 13:15

The Shape of Resilience

Resilience is a strange and holy thing.

You don't recognize it when life is calm.

You don't notice it when money flows, when plans behave, when the ground beneath you feels firm and loyal. You discover it when everything shifts, when the letter arrives with a whispering crack as it's opened, or when the door closes with an inevitable thud. In the dim kitchen, Marius clutches a mug, the steam curling upward, mingling with the cold air around him.

It isn't glamorous.

It doesn't shout.

It moves quietly.

Resilience is the stubborn act of breathing when existence feels airless.

It is the quivering hand still reaching for tomorrow.

It is the softly spoken thought beneath disappointment:

Not yet. I'm not finished.

Cornelius once said, "The strongest man is not the one who never falls, but the one who refuses to stay down."

Marius was on the verge of learning the truth of those words.

Marius's Breaking Point

Winter came early that year.

Not the postcard kind, but the extended, gray version, heavy and unkind.

In that season, Marius left his job.

It was steady, but it starved his soul.

He saved what he could, rented a modest space, and started a small business - nothing flashy, nothing reckless. Something honest.

For a moment, hope visited him.

A few customers.

A few encouraging words.

A few nights of tired hands and a brightened heart.

Then everything unraveled.

A supplier backed out.

Orders collapsed.

Money drained away.

One night, he sat in his dim kitchen, holding a worn mug for warmth.

His ledger spread open, red ink, circles, overdue notes.

Every number felt like a final decision.

“I can’t do this anymore,” he uttered.

But something inside answered back, quietly, stubbornly:

Not yet.

He remembered Cornelius’s words:

“With resilience, you don’t bounce back, you bend until you become something new.”

Maybe the goal wasn’t to return to who he used to be.

Maybe the goal was to grow into someone he had never been.

But the voice of failure grew loud:

You tried and failed again.

You should have stayed where you were.

Who did you think you were?

Beneath that voice, another rose - Cornelius’s voice:

“A fall doesn’t mean failure. It’s only a bend in the road. And bends lead to new horizons.”

That night, he sat long after the coffee cooled, between defeat and defiance, between "I'm done" and "Just once more."

The Young King and the Giant

Cornelius had previously told him about David, a shepherd boy underestimated by everyone.

A boy who faced lions and bears with no audience.

A boy mocked by his brothers.

A boy doubted by a king.

A boy cursed by a giant.

"But David," Cornelius said, "saw something different. He didn't see a giant blocking his future. He saw a chance to prove where his confidence truly lay."

David's victory did not come from weapons or size.

It came from conviction.

Back in his kitchen, Marius saw his own Goliath:

debt,

humiliation,

fear.

Resilience didn't mean pretending those giants weren't real.

It meant refusing to run from them.

That night, he closed the ledger.

He had no plan - but he had a decision.

He tore a piece of paper and wrote:

"Fall seven times, rise eight."

He pinned it to the wall.

And if you, dear reader, have reached your breaking point:

If money has vanished,

If trust has shattered,

If dreams lie in pieces - hear this:

You are not finished.

What broke you is not your definition, it is your preparation.

"Jehovah is close to the brokenhearted; He saves those who are crushed in spirit." **— Psalm 34:18**

One day, Marius would say:

"The storm doesn't end your journey, it clears the way for the sunrise."

But first, he had to live it.

The Law of Endurance

"Every storm has two winds. One breaks you. One builds you. Which one wins depends on your roots." Where does your deepest stability come from? Reflect on this question to understand your own 'roots' before the winds blow.

Resilience is not pretending.

It is moving through pain.

It is devotion to purpose while bleeding.

"The righteous one may fall seven times, and he will get up again." — **Proverbs 24:16**

Strength is not perfection; it is repetition.

Perseverance and Persistence

Cornelius told Marius, "Resilience has two children: perseverance and persistence."

Perseverance is the inner decision:

I will not quit.

Persistence is the outer action:

Watch what I do next.

Most people start strong and stop too soon.

They forget Jericho wasn't circled once, but seven times.

They forget King Jehoash struck the ground only three times - and lost the complete victory he could have had.

"Most men stop too soon," Cornelius said. "Heaven wasn't finished counting."

Keep striking.

The Lesson of Job

Job lost everything.

His home.

His children.

His wealth.

His health.

Even his friends turned into accusers.

Yet he said: "Though He slay me, I will still wait." **— Job 13:15**

Job didn't deny his pain; he poured it out.

But he refused to let suffering write his final chapter.

He came through the fire not unscarred - but refined.

The Blacksmith's Fire

One afternoon, Marius walked into a blacksmith's shop.

He watched glowing iron being struck again and again.

"You can't shape cold metal," the blacksmith said.

Marius finally understood that the fire wasn't punishment. It was a transformation.

Persistence in Modern Times

Cornelius spoke of:

- **Nelson Mandela -** twenty-seven years imprisoned, yet emerged ready to rebuild a nation
- **Helen Keller -** blind and deaf, yet emerged as an emblem of courage

- **Viktor Frankl -** discovered meaning inside the darkest human suffering
- The single mother working two jobs
- The teenager fighting invisible anxiety
- The elderly man planting a tree he will never sit under

"Resilience isn't rare," Cornelius said.

"It is the most human thing we have."

The Rebuilding Season

Marius began again - quietly.

He woke early.

He cleaned one drawer at a time.

He wrote every night:

What hurt me today?

What helped me today?

What healed me today?

Small steps.

little successes.

Small healings.

Resilience rarely appears in large displays.

It rises in stubborn, humble steps.

The Three Anchors of Resilience

1. Faith in A Higher Power

   "Jehovah will fight for you." — **Exodus 14:14**

   Faith does not silence the waves; it assures a shore beyond them.

2. Connection to Others

   "As iron sharpens iron, so one man sharpens his friend." — **Proverbs 27:17**

   No one endures alone.

   Not truly.

3. Focus on the Next Strike

   "He who watches the wind will not sow." — **Ecclesiastes 11:4**

   Waiting for perfect conditions is how decades disappear. Take the next honest step.

The Phoenix and the Seed

"The phoenix rises because it uses the fire," Cornelius said.

"The seed splits before it grows."

Breaking isn't always destruction; sometimes it is preparation.

The burial was planting.

Modern Parable of Hiroshi

Hiroshi, a Japanese craftsman, lost everything in the 2011 earthquake.

When asked how he could bear the loss, he said:

"The ground moved. So, I will move with it."

Resilience, Cornelius said,

is faith with hardened hands.

Reader Practice Session: Walking Through the Storm

Before continuing - pause.

This moment is yours.

These are gentle practices to help you stand while the storm continues to move around you.

1. Name Your Goliath

   Write:

   "This is the giant I am facing right now."

   Then answer honestly.

   Draw a line.

   Above it, write:

   "This is not my definition. This is my training ground."

2. Fall Seven Times, Rise Eight: Your Strength to Endure Inventory

   Draw three columns:

   Falls

   How I Got Back Up

   What I Learned

List three moments.

At the bottom write:

"With Jehovah's help, I have risen before. With His help, I will rise again."

3. Your Next Strike

Write:

"My next strike will be: _______."

Then add:

"I may feel afraid, but I will still move."

Place it where you'll see it.

4. The Three Anchors Check-In

Rate each from 1–10:

• My sense of God's nearness

• My connection to others

• My focus on the next small step

Strengthen the anchor with the lowest score.

5. A Prayer for the Brokenhearted

"Jehovah, you see what I carry, the weight, the fears, the broken pieces.

Strengthen my roots.

Hold my heart together when I cannot.

Teach me to rise again."

Place your hand over your heart. Feel its rhythm. Inhale slowly for a count of four, allowing the sensation to ground you in the present moment.

You are still here.

Closing Words of Chapter Eight

During an evening, Marius stood by his window.

The metropolitan lights flickered like scattered stars.

Life stirred around him - sirens, laughter, footsteps.

He thought of everything he lost.

Then everything he gained.

The miracle wasn't the disappearance of pain; it was his survival of it.

Cornelius had said,

"Do not pray for less pain, pray for stronger roots."

Marius whispered,

"I am still here."

That was his victory.

Resilience does not mean the storm never touched you.

It means you refused to become the storm.

"Every time you rise after falling," Cornelius said,

"Life itself stands to applaud."

And as Marius turned from the window, he understood:

The strength to stand was tied to one thing: the way he thought about his life, his God, his future, and himself.

The storm would come again.

But the perspective through which he saw it would determine whether he survived…or transformed.

And this is where the next lesson begins:

The Power of Thoughts and Attraction: When the Mind Begins to Shape the World.

Chapter Nine: The Power of Thoughts and Attraction

ൟ

"Your life expands or collapses according to the thoughts you allow to take root."

— Cornelius.

"Safeguard your heart, for out of it are the sources of life."

— Proverbs 4:23

"Whatever the mind of man can conceive and believe, it can achieve."

— Napoleon Hill

The Invisible Hand Behind Every Outcome

There is a law that governs success as surely as gravity governs the fall of a stone, known as the Law of Thought and Attraction. This law teaches us that the thoughts we cultivate shape the reality we experience. It is the invisible force that orchestrates the visible outcomes of our lives, silently steering every element of being.

It does not shout. It murmurs. Yet it moves everything you see.

Everything you call real - the chair beneath you, the walls around you, the technology you hold - began as a thought.

A flash in the invisible. A pattern in the unseen.

Before the world had buildings, men had blueprints in their minds.

Before flight existed, the dream of flight burned in the minds of those who refused to accept limitation.

The mind is the workshop of all creation - divine and human.

Thought is the architect. Faith is the builder. Action is the hand, the engineer, laying each stone.

The day Marius genuinely grasped the power of thought began quietly - almost too quietly.

It was late afternoon. A low sun pressed a warm golden hue against the city. The streets radiated soft copper light. Cafés hummed with casual conversation. A breeze pulled on the edges of newspapers spread across park benches. It was the kind of ordinary day that hides extraordinary truths.

Marius sat with Cornelius at their usual bench - the one overlooking the tender curve of the river. The older man watched the water thoughtfully, hands folded over the head of his cane.

"Look at the world around you," Cornelius said, sweeping his gaze slowly across the buildings, bridges, and busy people. "Every stone, every engine, every tower - none of it began in the quarry or factory. It began in here."

He tapped two fingers lightly against his temple.

Marius followed his gesture, absorbing the insight. The wooden seat below him was solid and cool. The lampposts lined the walkway. Even the phone alerting in his pocket - all once lived only as ideas.

"Thought," Cornelius continued, "is the architect. Faith is the builder. Action, the hand, the engineer - lays each stone."

Marius leaned back, watching a pair of joggers pass by.

"So, everything around us," he spoke in a low voice, "was once invisible?"

Cornelius smiled. "And now stands because someone believed enough to give it form."

"Every great engineering wonder begins in silence, not in the quarry, though in the stillness corner of a mind that dares to see what isn't yet."
— Cornelius.

The Magnetic Field of the Mind

Science tells us that every cell in the body vibrates with energy.

Faith tells us that belief is the current that forms that energy. Before accepting this principle on blind faith alone, take a moment to recall an instance in your own life when a change in mindset appeared to change your reality. Perhaps a moment when optimism opened unexpected doors, or when a shadow of doubt darkened opportunities. Such reflections become the foundation for comprehension of this: Together they point to a truth as old as creation itself - your thoughts are magnetic.

They attract to you the likeness of themselves.

When your mind is filled with doubt, it draws more reasons to doubt.

When you think in gratitude, you summon grace.

When you dwell on lack, opportunities hide.

But when you think abundance, life begins to respond with imprints of your own conviction.

"The mind is a magnet. It pulls toward it the metal of its making." — **Cornelius.**

The Experiment of Belief

On an evening, when Marius complained that nothing seemed to change despite his effort, Cornelius gave him what he called 'The Replacement Experiment.' For seven days, think only of what you wish to see, not what you are afraid of seeing. Every time a negative thought enters, replace it instantly with a picture of what you desire.

Marius agreed half-heartedly. He didn't expect much. But something extraordinary occurred.

On the second day, an old friend called him with a job lead.

On the third, a neighbor offered help with repairs.

By the seventh, he felt unburdened, more alive. The world hadn't changed - he had. And the world was only mirroring his new frequency.

"You didn't attract miracles. You stopped repelling them." **— Cornelius.**

The Law of Mental Correspondence

The ancients called it "As within, so without."

Hill called it autosuggestion.

Scripture calls it, "According to your faith let it happen to you." — **Matthew 9:29**

Whatever name you give it, the principle is the same:

You cannot attract into your life what you contradict in your mind.

You cannot seek peace while entertaining resentment.

You cannot call for love while speaking fear and hatred.

You cannot draw wealth while thinking of scarcity.

The universe does not respond to your words; it responds to your dominant vibration or mental attitude. To change your experience, you must first change your dominant inner atmosphere, your prevailing mental attitude. To change your experience, you must first change what you consistently think, feel, and rehearse.

Cornelius once compared the mind to a radio transmitter and explained:

Thoughts move outward like radio waves, carrying frequency and direction. They broadcast who you are becoming long before life reflects it to you. And like any signal, they attract what harmonizes at the same wavelength - people, opportunities, conflicts, and outcomes that mirror the mood you are sending.

This is why two people can walk through the same season and experience entirely different realities. One interprets challenge as proof of defeat. The other interprets it as evidence of growth. The circumstances may be identical, but the inner receiver is tuned differently.

Modern neuroscience now confirms what ancient wisdom long observed:

Our thoughts form perception, perception drives behavior, and behavior reinforces reality. Neural pathways strengthen where focus flows. The brain learns to find what the mind expects.

The Dialogue of Faith

When Marius once asked, "How can I believe in what I cannot see?" Cornelius answered,

"You already do. You believe the seed will become a tree, the dawn will follow the dark, the plane will rise into the sky. Why then do you doubt that your thoughts can rise into form?"

Faith is not blind optimism.

It is disciplined focus - choosing the higher thought again and again until it becomes second nature, until the soil of the mind is fertile enough for miracles to take root.

The Thought Garden

Cornelius once took Marius to a neglected garden behind his home.

Weeds had overrun the flowers.

"This," said Cornelius, "is a mind left unattended."

He knelt and began pulling the weeds, one by one.

You cannot grow roses in the same soil that nourishes thorns. Remember, every day you must choose what you allow to grow. As they say, weeds grow by default; flowers by decision.

He handed Marius a trowel.

"Now, start weeding."

The garden was not the lesson - the gardener was.

Cornelius explained it further in a way that kept the concept with Marius:

"The mind," he said, "as a garden, does not care what you *intend* to plant - it only grows what you *consistently sow.*"

Every thought is a seed.

Every repeated belief is a root.

Every emotion watered daily becomes a harvest.

Neglect the garden, and weeds do not ask permission.

Tend it intentionally, and even infertile ground can yield.

Start now, decide what you want your life to grow, and nurture it daily.

Modern Proof of Ancient Truth

Every invention, every breakthrough, every movement of progress is thought made visible.

When Thomas Edison failed a thousand times before inventing the lightbulb, he didn't call them failures - he called them discoveries.

When Oprah Winfrey was fired from her first TV job, she held to a vision of a higher purpose.

When Elon Musk was told rockets couldn't land themselves, he built one that did.

These are not superhuman tales. They are human stories driven by one common thread: the determined belief that what they saw in their minds could become flesh in the world. Persistence is not a passive hope; it is an active determination that connects vision and reality. Persistence is action-based faith, not wishful hoping. This is why Edison, Oprah, and Musk succeeded. They recognized that even though optimistic dreams, persistence gets to work.

"The difference between a dreamer and a creator is persistence in thought." **— Cornelius.**

The Mirror and the Echo

Modern neuroscience now confirms what ancient wisdom long observed:

Our thoughts form perception. Perception guides behavior; behavior reinforces reality. Neural pathways strengthen where focus repeatedly flows. The brain quite literally learns to look for what the mind expects to find.

In this way, the Law of Mental Correspondence functions like a mirror.

Life does not argue with your self-image.

It reflects it.

If you see yourself as powerless, the world will appear overwhelming.

If you see yourself as capable, the same world will present doors instead of obstacles.

If you carry unresolved fear, life will offer situations that awaken it.

If you cultivate faith, clarity, and expectancy, life will reflect them in form.

Cornelius put it simply:

"Life does not give you what you *want.*

It gives you what you *agree with* inside."

This is not punishment.

It is alignment.

And once Marius understood this, he realized something sobering and liberating all at once:

That he was far more than reacting to life, he was, in many unseen ways, *participating in its design.*

It dawned on him that life gives not what you demand, but what you reflect.

Your outer world is an emergence of your inner dialogue.

Angry thoughts return as conflict.

Grateful thoughts return as grace.

Fearful thoughts build walls.

Faithful thoughts open doors.

"You cannot curse the mirror and expect it to smile." **— Cornelius.**

Change the reflection, and the world adapts with you. Don't wait-choose now to align your thoughts with the outcomes you desire, and watch your world respond.

Practical Mastery - The Threefold Practice

Cornelius taught Marius a daily ritual called The Threefold Practice of Thought Mastery:

Morning Alignment:

Upon waking, spend five minutes visualizing how you want the day to unfold.

Speak aloud one affirmation of intent - "Today I walk in peace and purpose."

Midday Renewal

At noon, pause. Notice your dominant thoughts.

If they've drifted toward fear or frustration, gently guide them back to gratitude.

Night Reflection:

Before sleep, review the day.

Give thanks for progress, forgive the rest, and picture tomorrow brighter still.

"Do this for thirty days," said Cornelius, "and watch the world bend subtly toward your new vibration."

The Biblical Blueprint

From the beginning, the Creator demonstrated the divine pattern of manifestation:

"And God said, 'Let there be light,' then there was light." **— Genesis 1:3**

Creation began not with labor, but with thought spoken into form.

You, made in that same image, share that pattern - the ability to think, to speak, to act, and thus to create.

"To think rightly is to participate in divine creation." **— Cornelius**

The Warning of Neglected Thought

Thought is power, but power unguarded becomes dangerous.

Fear, resentment, and self-pity are weeds that strangle the garden.

Marius asked, "Can thoughts destroy?"

Cornelius answered softly,

"They can - when you forget that you are their master."

Worry and envy are prayers sent in the wrong direction.

They feed what you dread.

If you do not choose your thoughts, someone or something else will - and life will mirror their disorder instead of your purpose.

Faith, Focus, and Flow

Faith is not passive belief - it is active cooperation with prospect.

Focus is its twin, keeping the mind fixed on what it seeks rather than what it fears.

Together, they create flow - the effortless momentum that arises when thought, word, and action move in harmony.

"The world does not bend to your will - it bends to your awareness." **— Cornelius.**

Exercise - The Thought Ledger

Each night, take a journal and draw two columns: Fear and Faith.

Under Fear, write every anxious thought that visited you today.

Under Faith, write the truth that counters it.

Example:

"I may fail." → "Every step forward is growth."

"I'm alone." → "Help and friendship await those who seek them."

Do this daily. You will see which side wins by repetition - and that awareness alone will begin to shift your mind toward victory.

Closing Words of Chapter Nine

Every man lives in two worlds - the world of matter and the world of mind.

The latter shapes the former.

Guard your inner speech.

Sow good seed daily.

Choose thoughts worthy of the life you desire.

Because every blessing, every opportunity, every turn of fortune begins the same way - as a single, quiet, faithful thought.

"The universe listens not to noise, but to conviction." **— Cornelius.**

Chapter Ten: The Power of Perspective and Action - Changing the Lens That Shapes Your World

❧

"You cannot change the horizon, but you can climb higher to see it differently."

— Cornelius.

"Do not wait: the time will never be 'just right.' Start where you stand."

— Napoleon Hill

"For now, we see in hazy outline by means of a metal mirror, but then it will be face-to-face. At present, I know partially, but then I will know accurately."

— 1 Corinthians

13:12

The Tilt of the Lens

One morning, Marius sat beside Cornelius on a low stone wall overlooking the fog-veiled town. The environment felt damp and metallic on his tongue; the early light had not yet made up its mind. The Empire State Building's pinnacle, tall and sure on clear days, was now lost in a blanket of mist.

Cornelius's coat collar was turned up facing the chill. For a long time, he said nothing, just watched the gray blanket hanging over the city as though weighing it.

Then, without turning his head, he asked quietly,

"Tell me, what do you see?"

"A city swallowed by fog," Marius said. His voice bore the flatness of someone who had long grown used to bad weather in the soul.

Cornelius reached into his pocket, pulled out a small, mildly dulled mirror, and handed it to him. Then, with a deliberate motion, he tilted it toward the sky. In its reflection, Marius caught a sudden, startling glimpse of sunlight above the clouds - bright, clean, unaffected by the gloom below.

"Perspective," Cornelius said. His tone was gentle, but there was a sharpness underneath it, like iron beneath velvet. "It does not change the facts - it changes how much of the truth you can see."

The words impacted harder than usual. Cornelius's eyes were far from kind; for a moment, they were intense, searching Marius's face as if testing how much he was willing to understand.

That morning, Marius learned that the fog is not the problem; the altitude of your sight is. Thinking about this, he began to wonder: What has fog-level sight already cost you this week? By naming a real loss, Marius found himself desiring the clarity that comes with a higher view.

The Prison of Perception

Most men live behind invisible bars, the limits of their own perception. They call it "reality," but often it is only habit: the mind's decision to look through the same window, in the same direction, every single day. What is one 'I always' story you tell yourself that keeps you confined in this self-imposed prison? Interrupting that narrative loop can be the key to breaking free and widening your horizon.

Two people can face the same circumstance. One sees doom; the other, destiny. The difference is not the condition - it is the vision.

Marius previously believed that life happened to him. Problems appeared like the weather. Pain came like unpaid bills. He had seen himself as a passenger, forced to sit through scenes he never chose.

Cornelius helped him see that life happens through you, as you see it.

"Your eyes," the old man once said, "are not just receivers. They are interpreters. They don't just report what is - they decide what it means."

Marius began to realize that his greatest prison had never been the job, the debt, or the failures. It had been his own rigid way of seeing.

The Parable of the Two Salesmen

One afternoon, Cornelius straightened up from the bench with a wince in his back - a prompt that even wise men age - then turned to Marius with an expression that was unusually sharp, almost urgent.

"Listen carefully," he said. "Because how you see this will follow you for the rest of your life."

He told him the story of two shoe salesmen sent by a factory to a distant island.

"When they arrived," Cornelius said, "they found that no one on the island wore shoes."

He raised a hand, emphasizing each word.

"The first salesman sent this message to headquarters:

"Returning home. No one wears shoes."

He paused a beat, then continued.

"But the second sent a different message:

"Send all available stock. No one wears shoes - no competition!"

Cornelius turned fully toward Marius now, his fixed gaze.

"The same island. The same people. The same situation. Yet one saw hopelessness; the other, a horizon. Imagine, Marius, that the island holds 10,000 potential customers. Realizing this turns abstract optimism into a tangible opportunity."

He leaned in a little closer.

"Life doesn't decide what it means, you do. One man retreats; another advances. Both are right - according to their sight."

For once, there was almost a rebuke in Cornelius's tone - not cruel, though steadfast, like a father refusing to let a child keep hurting himself the same way.

Marius swallowed. It wasn't a story anymore. It acted as a mirror.

The Story of Joseph and the Twelve Spies

Later, while they strolled a quiet street lined with bare trees, Cornelius drew Marius back to a familiar figure - Joseph.

"Imagine him," Cornelius said, "alone in prison after betrayal. The iron, the stench, the silence. He could have called himself forsaken, and from that angle, he would've been right. Or he could believe that even this cell was a classroom - and that, too, would've been true."

Joseph's life did not change when he left prison. It changed when he saw the prison as preparation. The same walls that confined him became the womb of his purpose.

"Remember me when things go well with you…mention me to Pharaoh, to get me out of this place." **— Genesis 40:14**

Cornelius's voice mellowed, then hardened again with emphasis.

"Now, Joseph was not the only one tested by perception. The children of Israel were, too."

He told Marius the story of the twelve spies sent into Canaan.

"All twelve saw the same land - fertile, rich, overflowing with promise. Ten came back trembling. They said, 'The people whom we saw in it are men of extraordinary size; in comparison, we seemed like grasshoppers, both to them."

His hand clenched on the handle of his cane.

"Two - Caleb and Joshua - came back burning with courage. They said, 'Nevertheless, the people who dwell in the land are strong, and the fortified cities are very great - Let us go up immediately to take possession of it, because we can surely conquer it."**— Numbers 13:28-33.**

He turned abruptly to face Marius, his eyes radiant and fierce.

"The ten saw obstacles. The two saw an opportunity. And their reports determined their destiny. The ten never entered the land they feared; the two inherited the promise they believed."

Cornelius's tone lowered, but the intensity remained.

"Joseph saw beyond his prison. Caleb and Joshua saw beyond their giants. The eye of faith sees preparation where others see punishment."

The moral was clear - and this time, it didn't drift in gently. It pressed.

What you call defeat may be the ground where victory is waiting to bloom.

The Two Windows of the Mind

One pleasant evening, Cornelius led Marius down a quiet alley between two weathered houses. The stones underfoot were slippery with the day's earlier rain, glistening in the pale orange from a lone streetlamp.

There were two windows, side by side, each looking into a different world.

Through one, the view was harsh - broken barrels, tangled weeds, rusted tools, and walls covered in the graffiti of neglect. The glass itself was cloudy, marked with fingerprints and old rain.

Through the other, a field of wildflowers sparkled beneath the setting sun, and fireflies danced like sparks of promise rising from the earth. The air on that side carried a subtle scent of cut grass and distant blossoms.

"Which would you rather wake to each morning?" Cornelius asked.

Marius didn't hesitate. "The field, of course."

Cornelius nodded - but this time his speech was firm, almost commanding.

"Then open that window. Every day begins with a choice - which window you open, and which you keep shut. Peace is not found in the view, but in the direction, you choose to face."

They stood there when twilight descended, the alley wrapped in a soft hum of far-off traffic and the occasional bark of a dog. Marius understood at that moment that life, too, offered these two windows - one filled with everything broken, and the other, with everything still beautiful.

Cornelius later told him,

"The mind is a camera. Whatever you focus on, you develop. Keep it fixed on fear, and your world grows darker. Turn it toward gratitude, and even night begins to glow."

That evening, Marius began a quiet discipline - not to change the world, but to change the way he looked at it.

When plans were delayed, he saw the virtue of patience in training.

When others judged him, he saw a chance to grow steadier.

When loneliness visited, he called it preparation for an enhanced rapport.

The city around him hadn't changed - the noise, the traffic, the endless demands. Yet something in him had risen above it. The same streets that had once felt like a cell began to feel like passageways of purpose.

One morning, Cornelius took him up a steep hill overlooking the valley. The climb was long, and halfway up, Marius stopped, gasping for breath.

"It looks no different from here," he said between breaths.

Cornelius looked back at him, look intensifying with a trace of impatience - gentle, though insistent.

"Then climb higher," he said.

No soft chuckle, without softness diversion - just a clear command.

When they arrived at the peak, the fog below began to thin, and the town stretched out beneath them - not dull and gray, but bathed in gold. The rooftops glimmered like scales of light, the same city now seen from a higher place.

Cornelius turned to him and said quietly, but with a gravity which created every word sense weighty,

"The problem was never the path - it was the height. The higher you rise, the clearer the pattern becomes. What once looked like punishment begins to reveal itself as preparation."

Marius watched the sun spill over the roofs and fields below, and he finally understood.

Life does not always change its scenery, but it will always change its meaning for those who dare to climb higher, to look longer, and to choose the window of gratitude over the window of gloom.

Cornelius rested his hand on Marius's shoulder, his grip firmer than usual.

"Remember," he said, "every morning gives you two windows. One shows what you've lost. The other shows what remains. Open wisely - for your peace will follow your gaze."

The Law of Interpretation

Cornelius once told Marius, "Everything that happens to you carries two messages - one written in ink, and one in light. The first, you read too quickly; the second, you must wait to see."

Every experience, he explained, has two interpretations - the immediate and the eternal.

The immediate is born of reaction - it shouts, complains, rushes to judgment.

The eternal is born of reflection - it murmurs, listens, and waits to grasp to ripen.

The first interpretation makes a man bitter.

The second makes him better.

"Be quick to see," Cornelius would say, "but slow to conclude. Wisdom isn't new eyes - it's learning to look longer before deciding what you see."

Sometimes, when he said this, there was a trace of force in his expression - as if he knew how much harm a rushed conclusion could cause.

Marius learned that truth the hard way.

After his early failures, he often looked back and cursed the instances when he had broken him - the lost opportunities, the betrayals, the long stretches of silence when nothing seemed to work.

He called them wasted years.

But as time passed, he came to realize things differently.

Those same years had also refined him, teaching patience where pride once ruled, depth where haste once lived. He realized that what had looked like a delay was, in fact, a design.

It was Cornelius who helped him understand this shift.

"Events themselves are neutral," the old man said at a certain twilight. The setting sun carved hard lines across his face, and for once, he looked every year of his age. "It is your interpretation that gives them power. You can see the rain as an interruption or as irrigation. You can call the waiting a punishment or preparation. What changes life isn't what happens - but how you read it."

Marius inclined his head slowly. It was another lesson in shortening the day.

When you rush to interpret, the day grows longer with frustration and self-pity.

But when you pause - when you let meaning unfold in its own hour - peace enters the room, and the day becomes lighter, shorter, more bearable.

Cornelius once compared interpretation to tending a garden.

“If you dig up the seed every day to see if it’s growing,” he said, his speech suddenly sharp with warning, “you’ll kill it. Let it rest beneath the soil. Give it time. Only then will it reveal what it was meant to become.”

The same is true of life’s trials.

When pain strikes, the first reaction is always confusion - “Why this? Why now?”

But if you hold steady, if you trust that time will unveil its reason, the sharp edge of suffering begins to soften into understanding.

Even Scripture carries this wisdom. “We see through a glass, darkly,” wrote Paul - meaning that our view of life is incomplete, clouded by haste and emotion. Only patience brings clarity.

Cornelius once leaned back and said, “Marius, meaning never shouts - it waits for the mind that has grown quiet enough to hear.” There was a tiredness in that admission, as though he knew how many people go to their graves without ever listening.

He taught him that interpretation is not the art of explaining what happened; it is the discipline of finding purpose within it.

It is the quiet mastery of perspective - the power to transform a wound into wisdom, a delay into direction, and a discouragement into divine timing.

When you learn this, your days no longer seem infinite with confusion.

Each one becomes a page in a story you can finally read - slowly, purposefully, gratefully.

The Mirror of Gratitude

"Gratitude," Cornelius once told Marius, "Is the mirror that changes how you see the world - not by altering the reflection, but by teaching you to recognize the light."

Gratitude has a strange kind of power. It doesn't erase pain; it redeems it.

It doesn't pretend storms are sunshine; it teaches you to dance even in the rain.

When Marius asked Cornelius how to keep his heart steady when all seemed broken, the old man's expression changed. The usual softness in his eyes tightened into something fiercer.

"If you can't find the blessing," he said, "look again."

The words were not a suggestion. They were a command, spoken with a sudden urgency that startled Marius.

At first, he didn't understand. But as he began to practice it - to search, even in loss, for one small reason to be thankful - he discovered that the very act of looking started to mend him.

Gratitude is the fastest way to shift perspective. It's the switch that flips scarcity into sufficiency, despair transforming into direction.

When you start counting what remains instead of what's gone, abundance begins to grow where lack once lived.

Paul once wrote, "In everything give thanks."

Not for everything - for no one is expected to celebrate heartbreak or betrayal - but in everything. Even in the dark, gratitude becomes the candle that helps you see.

Cornelius called it "finding the silver thread through the tangle."

He told Marius, "Gratitude is not denial. It is defiance - the decision to keep seeing beauty where others see only ruin."

It takes courage to be grateful when life doesn't cooperate, when plans fail, when people disappoint. But gratitude is not naïve; it is wise. It knows there is always a bigger picture, even when your corner of the canvas looks chaotic.

When you give thanks in the midst of struggle, you reclaim your authority over it.

You stop being the victim of what happened and become the author of what it means.

That is the real miracle of gratitude - it turns every difficulty into soil, every loss into a lesson, every moment into meaning.

Cornelius often reminded Marius,

"The man who learns to give thanks in the middle of a storm doesn't escape the storm - he masters it."

Sometimes he said it softly. But as the years drew on, there came days when he said it with a fire in the tone he used, as if he needed Marius to remember it for a time when he himself would no longer be there to repeat it.

The Inverted Map

One quiet afternoon, Marius came upon Cornelius sitting below the aged oak, studying an upside-down map.

The leaves above them hushed in the breeze. A few dry ones fluttered across the path like unsettled thoughts.

"Why do you read it like that?" Marius asked, amused.

Cornelius did not chuckle this time. His lips quivered, but his eyes stayed serious.

"Because sometimes you must turn the map to see roads invisible from the usual direction."

At first, Marius thought he was joking. But as he watched, the old man drew a line with his finger, paused, and nodded, as if something hidden had suddenly revealed itself.

"Life," Cornelius uttered quietly, yet with a kind of tired insistence, "works the same way. When you're lost, don't curse the path - turn the map."

That night, Marius couldn't shake those words.

He had been roaming through his own maze of confusion - plans that had failed, dreams that no longer fit, prayers that appeared unanswered. He realized he had been walking in circles, just as a hiker might do in the thick of the woods, tracing the same ground again and again, hoping it would lead somewhere new.

Then he remembered the story Cornelius once told him.

"There was a woman," the old man said, "a hiker who had lost her way in the forest. She walked for hours, exhausted, unsure where to go. Every path looked the same. Finally, she stopped, pulled out her map, and stared at it until her hope began to fade. But in a last attempt, she flipped the map upside down - and suddenly, the landmarks made sense. She saw a trail that had always been there, one she'd overlooked because she was facing the wrong way. When she followed it, she found her way out."

Cornelius paused when he'd first told that story, his mouth set firmly.

"The path was always there," he said. "The problem wasn't the forest, it was the direction she was facing."

That image stayed with Marius like an engraving on the heart. He saw himself in that hiker - weary, disoriented, trying to find one's way in life through the same lens that had led him in circles.

Sometimes, the breakthrough doesn't come from doing more, but from seeing differently.

This, Cornelius explained, was the art of shortening the day. It was not the act of shrinking time, but of simplifying the gaze - of seeing clearly what matters most in the present moment, instead of being blinded by the expanse of everything at once.

Perspective, he said, does not create a new road - it reveals the one that has been waiting all along.

Cornelius loved to illustrate this point with the story of the prophet Elisha. He once told Marius how an enemy army surrounded Elisha and his servant. The young servant panicked, certain they were doomed. But Elisha prayed, "Lord, open his eyes that he may see."

And when his eyes were opened, he saw that they had company - the hills around them were filled with horses and chariots of fire.

Cornelius moved nearer that day, his quiet tone but intense.

"Your enemies may not vanish, Marius, but your vision can change. The moment you see differently, the battle itself begins to lose its power."

Marius recognized then that the true enemy was not the storm, but blindness - the inability to recognize that also in chaos, there is direction.

When you feel trapped in a long day of confusion, when every road looks the same, turn the map. Rethink the problem. Revisit your beliefs. Sometimes, what you call the end of the road is only the beginning of another one, waiting for the courage of a different view.

For the road has always been there; it's the eyes that must learn to see it.

From Sight to Motion

Seeing differently is not enough; you must move differently. Perspective opens the mind. Action opens the world. To translate this shift in perspective into a tangible step, begin a simple, ten-minute task. For instance, at the end of the day, reframe one setback in your journal. Write down the challenge and, beside it, list a potential benefit or lesson it holds. Linking perspective to immediate action reinforces the sight-to-motion thesis.

"The universe rewards movement, not meditation alone," he said.

He paused, then added an illustration Marius would never forget.

"Have you ever tried to steer a parked carriage?" he asked.

Marius grinned softly. "No."

"You cannot," Cornelius said. This time, his voice bore a harder edge. "The wheels must turn before direction is possible. A stationary vehicle can be polished, admired, and prayed over - but until it moves, the driver holds no power over its path."

He looked toward the winding road beyond the garden, jaw set, as if he were staring down an enemy only he could see.

"So it is with life," he continued. "God can guide a moving soul far more easily than a still one. Faith may be the ignition, but motion is the steering. Start moving, and you will find that heaven begins to nudge the wheel."

Faith changes your vision.

Action fulfills it.

The Lamp and the Path

During one evening, Cornelius handed Marius a small oil lamp. Its light twinkled softly, barely strong enough to reach the garden road ahead. The air carried the faint scent of soil and smoke.

"Walk," the old man said.

Marius hesitated. "But the lamp is too dim. It shows only a few steps."

Cornelius's expression tightened slightly.

"Then take those few steps," he replied, "and the next will appear."

He turned away, adding in a tone mild yet firm, "Illumination follows initiative. Each act of courage lights another foot of the path."

Marius looked down at the trembling flame. It seemed almost foolish - one fragile light against the shadowy stretch of the garden. Yet, as he began to walk, something astonishing took place. With every step, the route ahead brightened just enough for the next.

He recognized then that life works the same way. We wait for the whole road to unfold before we move, but the light never comes to the man who stands still. It comes to the one who dares to begin.

Cornelius once compared this lesson to the words of the Psalmist:

"Your word is a lamp to my foot, and a light for my path." **— Psalm 119:105**

The verse, he said, does not promise a floodlight for the miles ahead - only a lamp for the next few steps. That is the rhythm of faith.

"Those who demand to see the whole road before moving," Cornelius told him, "Never leave their doorstep. But the one who takes the first uncertain step invites the dawn."

A few nights later, as they sat near the fire, Marius remembered the story Cornelius had told him weeks ago - the story of King Jehoash and the arrows.

"I finally understand why the king failed," Marius said quietly. "He struck the ground three times and stopped. He stopped because he couldn't see the outcome. He didn't trust that the motion itself was creating the victory."

Cornelius nodded, but this time the agreement came with a sharp trace of passion.

"Exactly," he said. "He had the weapon and the instruction, but he lacked the persistence to strike in the dark. The man who keeps striking, even when he cannot see the wall breaking, is the one who eventually breaks through."

The next day, Marius found himself considering another of Cornelius's sayings:

"Perspective gives clarity. Action gives momentum. Together, they give transformation."

The words came across as a secret law of life, one that ruled every change he'd ever witnessed.

To see clearly is noble.

To move upon what is seen is divine.

A thought left unacted is a seed unplanted. It will never grow.

He remembered Cornelius writing on a scrap of paper:

"The world changes for the man who changes the way he sees, and then acts on what he sees."

That truth had influenced the lives of those who dared to combine vision with movement.

Thomas Edison saw light in failure, not darkness in defeat. Thousands of experiments that others called mistakes became his stepping stones to invention.

Nelson Mandela saw reconciliation as others perceived revenge. From the walls of his prison, he built a bridge that healed a nation.

Both men looked into the same darkness that others feared, and declared, "There is something more here."

Marius began to recognize that all life has its own lamp and its own path. The lamp is faith - the willingness to take the next step. The path is purpose, revealed one act at a time.

The man who waits for certainty remains in the dark. The one who walks in trust finds his light expanding at every pace.

Cornelius had said it best:

"The lamp may tremble, the road may twist, but the man who keeps walking will always find the dawn."

When he said it that time, there was a catch in the tone of his voice. For a swift instant, Marius had the odd feeling that Cornelius was simply not teaching him a principle, but bequeathing him a final instruction.

The Daily Practice - The Climb and the Step

In the ensuing days, Cornelius left Marius with what he called The Daily Climb. He spoke the words slowly, carefully, as though carving them into the younger man's memory.

"Listen to me now," he said, eyes radiant with a sudden, almost fierce urgency. "These four habits will hold you when I no longer can."

Rise and Reframe

Before leaving bed, choose which window to open - gratitude or grievance.

See and Step.

Visualize your purpose, then act before hesitation intervenes.

Climb Higher.

When doubt clouds your view, raise your mind, not your excuses.

Record the View.

Each evening, write one thing you saw differently and one thing you did because of it.

"Vision without movement is illusion," said Cornelius. "Movement without vision is chaos. But together - they move the world."

Marius sensed the burden in the old man's voice. It was no longer advice; it was legacy.

Closing Words of Chapter Ten

Life hardly ever changes its scenery - the same streets, the same routines, the same familiar faces. Yet those who live with awakened eyes know that life doesn't have to change around them for something within them to shift entirely.

The difference in the midst of despair and discovery is often only a matter of sight.

A man who sees with fear finds obstacles at every turn.

But a man who learns to see with thankfulness, with faith, and with purpose - finds paths hidden in plain view.

Cornelius once told Marius,

"When you can no longer change the wind, adjust the sails. The same storm that breaks one ship carries another home."

Perspective, when joined with motion, becomes transformation.

Every step you take in light - even if that light shows only the next few feet - is an act of faith.

And faith, when practiced daily, reshapes the entire landscape before you.

The world may not grow easier. The road may not grow smoother. But you will grow steadier, clearer, and stronger. And soon, the same day that previously felt too long begins to feel packed - full of possibility, full of meaning, full of quiet miracles hidden within ordinary hours.

So, keep your lamp trimmed. Keep your vision lifted. Keep walking toward what is good, true, and beautiful.

For, as Cornelius said:

"Most people wait for the world to brighten before they open their eyes. But those who open their eyes first - they bring the dawn."

Chapter Eleven: Living with Intention - The Compass and the Clock

❧

"A man without intention moves like a ship without a captain. He floats, but he never arrives."

— Cornelius.

"If one does not know to which port one is sailing, no wind is favorable."

— Seneca.

"Do you know that the runners in a race all run, but only one receives the prize? Run in such a way that you may win it."

— 1 Corinthians 9:24

The Burden of a Rushed Day

The city was only half awake.

The park was quiet under the cold, blue pre-dawn. Streetlights lingered as frost glazed the grass.

Marius sat on the bench, elbows on knees, fingers laced tight.

He had known despair before. He had sat in this park under the crushing load of failure, of debt, of grief.

This was different.

This time, it wasn't the numbness of lost hope.

Now, he felt the restless discomfort of someone who had found purpose yet still seemed to be sinking.

Now, the community center buzzed with new programs and faces.

More calls. More messages.

Requests for help.

People to meet.

Forms to file.

A board to report to.

His phone vibrated: reminders, emails, updates - a constant signal that he was behind.

He wasn't failing now.

He was busy.

But now, endless activity pressed heavier than past failures ever had.

"Shorten the day," he spoke quietly to himself, repeating the first lesson. "One thing at a time. One meaningful thing…"

But already his mind rushed to calls, meetings, grants, bills, and an unanswered message from his sister.

He had never been more purposeful, yet his chest was tight, thoughts all over the place.

He wondered again, why does the day still feel too long - and yet never enough?

Footsteps stepped on the gravel path behind him.

Without looking up, he knew.

"Your shoulders are back to carrying more than one day at a time," Cornelius said.

Marius glanced sideways.

The old man stood, coat buttoned, scarf tucked, vapor rising from the cup in his gloved hand. For the first time, Marius noticed not just calm but a firm intensity in his eyes, like a warning bell quietly ringing.

"You're early," Marius said.

Cornelius lowered himself onto the bench with a slight exhale. "So are you. And so is whatever you're trying to outrun."

They sat in silence for a moment, watching a lone jogger make his way around the path, breath pulsing, floating through the air like a steady drumbeat.

After a long silence, Marius finally said,

"I thought purpose would make life easier. Instead, I'm always behind, falling asleep with things unfinished, waking up rushed."

He shook his head.

"It's like my life finally has meaning - and that meaning is crushing me."

Cornelius nodded once, slowly.

"There is a sickness," he spoke quietly, softly, "that afflicts men who finally care about their days. I've been waiting for it to find you."

Marius turned to him. "What sickness?"

The old man looked straight ahead, jaw set.

The disease of hurry," Cornelius said. "The quiet cancer of comparison. The tyranny of the Clock."

The Tyranny of the Urgent

Marius frowned. "I thought urgency was good. You told me not to waste days."

Cornelius took a measured breath, choosing his words with care.

"Urgency," he said, "has its place. When the house is on fire, you run. When a man is bleeding, you don't sit down and draft a plan, you press your hands into the wound."

He turned, and for the first time since Marius had known him, the expression he used intensified.

"But you, Marius, are living as though every hour is a house on fire."

The words cut. Not because they were cruel, but because they were true.

Cornelius tapped his cane against the gravel.

"You have confused urgency with importance," he said. "You are letting other people's noise set the rhythm of your soul. That is why your day feels too long and too short at the same time, long in pressure, short in meaning."

Marius stared at the ground, lost in thought.

"I don't know how to stop. Someone always needs me; something's late. If I slow down, everything unravels."

Cornelius studied him, saying nothing for a moment.

Then, without a word, he leaned forward and began tracing two circles in the dirt with the tip of his cane.

The Compass and the Clock

"The world," Cornelius said, "has given you this."

He tapped the first circle - a rough ring in the gravel.

"The Clock."

He drew little lines around it, like rays on a sun.

"The Clock is loud," he said. "It's like an alarm always blaring, demanding your attention. The Clock measures how busy you are - how fast you answer, how quickly you do things, how much activity you squeeze into an hour. It's the outside world pushing you to move faster, always counting time, but not caring where you're actually going."

He paused.

"It does not care where you are going, only how quickly you move."

He shifted the cane to the second circle.

"And this," he said in a low voice, "is the Compass."

He shaded this one in, a small dark center with a single arrow pointing north.

"The Compass is quiet," he said. "Picture it as an inner guide, softly helping you choose your direction. While the Clock is about speed, the Compass cares about whether you're moving in the right direction. It helps you decide if your actions today match your values, who you are, and what truly matters to you in this moment."

Cornelius sat back, letting his words settle.

"Your pain is simple: you've built days around the Clock, but your soul needs the Compass."

Marius watched the two circles, the lines of the Clock, the arrow of the Compass.

"So what does that mean?" he asked.

Cornelius's expression changed again. There was no tender smile now - only deep seriousness.

It means that you are letting the world tell you how fast to move, instead of allowing wisdom tell you where to move, direction before speed.

He fixed Marius with a look that did not waver.

"When you carry time, it burdens you. When you give time direction, it blesses you."

The words registered in Marius like a key turning.

He realized that lately, his days had not been framed by one clear intention, but by the noise of other people's demands.

Emails. Messages. Expectations.

All urgency. Little intention.

"How do I live by the Compass? What does that look like in a real day?"

Cornelius's eyes relaxed, yet the haste within them did not fade.

"First," he said, "you must understand the enemy of the Compass."

The Law of Comparison

They walked slowly along the path, leaving the two circles behind them. The sky had grown calmer now, streaks of pale gold leaking across the horizon.

"Tell me," Cornelius said, "when does your peace leave you the fastest?"

Marius didn't have to think long.

"When I look around," he said. "When I see what others are doing. How far they've come. How quickly they move. It's like I'm running a race I never signed up for."

Cornelius nodded.

"The Clock," he said, "rarely works alone. It brings a cruel accomplice wherever it goes."

He stopped walking and faced Marius.

"Comparison."

Marius said nothing. He didn't need to. The word itself hit a nerve.

Cornelius continued.

"There's an old story," he said, "about workers hired for a vineyard."

His voice lowered, edged with gravity.

"The owner went out at dawn and hired workers for a fair wage. They were content. They went to the field gladly. Hours later, he hired more men. Near evening, he hired a few more. When the day was done, he paid them all the same."

Marius inclined his head gently. He knew the parable - but he had never heard it told like this.

"The ones hired first," Cornelius said, "were not angry until they saw the others get paid."

He looked straight into Marius's eyes.

"Do you see? Their joy collapsed not when they labored…but when they looked sideways."

He allowed silence to sit for a moment.

"A man," Cornelius said quietly, "can lose a lifetime of contentment in a single sideways glance."

The words cut straight through the fog in Marius's mind.

He thought of the nights he scrolled on his phone, measuring his slow progress against other people's best moments. He thought of the instances he felt proud of a small win… until he saw someone else's bigger one.

"Comparison," Cornelius went on, "is the thief of gratitude. It steals not your opportunities, but your joy in the ones you already have."

He began walking again, slower now.

"You were at peace when you were simply grateful to labor in your vineyard," he said. "Now you are counting other men's wages."

Marius swallowed. The truth hurt.

"So how do I stop?" he asked. "How do I stop looking sideways?"

Cornelius stopped under a bare-branched tree, took a breath, and turned to him with a seriousness Marius had never seen before.

"By learning," he said, "to look at the right thing first."

The Mirror and the Window

Cornelius pointed his cane toward the apartments across the street, lights blinking on one by one as the city woke.

"Every morning," he said, "most men do the same foolish thing."

He raised a hand and mimed pulling a curtain aside.

"They go straight to the window."

He held his hand there, as though frozen in the act.

"They look at the world before they have looked at themselves. News, messages, social feeds - all through the window. The Window lets in everything from outside, rushing in and scattering your own purposes before you've set them. But the Mirror is different: it's about looking inward first, finding your intent before reacting to the world."

He dropped his hand.

"The wise man," Cornelius said, "polishes the mirror first."

Marius pictured his own mornings: waking, reaching for his phone before his feet touched the floor, scanning other people's urgency, opinions, emergencies… and only then remembering his own purpose.

"What does it mean to polish the mirror?" he asked.

Cornelius's voice slowed. Each word carried weight.

"It means," he said, "that before you expose your heart to the world's demands, you ask three quiet questions in the stillness of your own soul."

He held up one finger.

"First: Who am I becoming? Not what do I have to do = who am I, actually, turning into?"

Second finger.

"Second: What truly matters today? Not what is loudest, not what is urgent - what is important?"

Third finger.

"Third: What is my one intention? One. Not ten. Not twenty-seven tasks. One thread that gives the day a spine."

He paused.

"A man with a clear mirror," he said, "can look through any window without losing himself." To put this philosophy into practice, consider setting a micro-challenge for yourself tomorrow morning.

Before you check your phone, take a moment for intention by delaying that action by five deep breaths. Use this time to focus on who you want to become today, what really matters, and your one intention for the day. This experiment can help you to start forming the habit of living deliberately, with a clear mind and a purposeful heart.

He stepped a little closer, his tone tightening.

"But when the mirror is fogged, the window will lie to you."

Marius frowned. "How can a window lie?"

Cornelius's eyes flashed.

"Because if you approach the world unclear, the world will gladly tell you who you are, what you should want, and how far behind you are."

The sound of the expression he used, for the first time since the park seat in their earliest meeting, grew sharp.

"Listen to me, Marius."

The command in his tone made Marius straighten unconsciously.

"If you do not set your intention before you open the window, the world will sell you one. And it will never be aligned with your soul."

The old man's hand quivered lightly on the cane - not with weakness, but with emphasis.

"You must learn," he said, "to master your pauses. The space between waking and reacting. The holy seconds before your attention is captured. In those pauses, destinies are decided."

The Four Faces of Patience

They had reached the far end of the park now, where the path narrowed and a small stream cut through the grass, whispering over worn stones.

Cornelius slowed his steps.

"Intention," he said, "is not only about where you point your life. It is about how you walk it."

He glanced sideways at Marius.

"You move as if everything depends on your speed. But if you wish to live by the Compass, you must learn the art of patience."

Marius almost laughed. "I'm not sure patience is my gift."

Cornelius gave a short chuckle.

"Patience," he said, "is not a gift. It is a discipline."

He lifted his cane and gestured slightly, as if outlining an invisible frame in the air.

"Scripture says to clothe yourself with patience," he uttered. "You don't wake up wearing it, you put it on."

He raised one finger again.

"A patient man is slow to anger," he said. "He stays calm under stress. When others rush him, he does not bite. He breathes."

Second finger.

"A patient man can wait calmly," he continued. "When something takes longer than expected, he does not let irritation poison the whole day."

Third finger.

"A patient man is not rash. When he has an important task, he does not sprint through it. He chooses quality over speed."

Fourth finger.

"And a patient man endures trials without constant complaint," Cornelius finished. "He may feel the weight - he will - but he carries it with a quiet strength that does not infect everyone around him."

He lowered his hand.

"These four," he said, "are the clothes of a man who lives by the Compass, not the Clock."

Marius thought of his last month, sharp replies, rushed decisions, heavy sighs that filled rooms, the tightness in his chest as he hurried from one task to another.

"I haven't been wearing patience," he uttered calmly.

"You've been wearing panic," Cornelius replied.

There was no judgment in his tone, only a calm diagnosis.

"But panic is a costume," he added. "It does not belong to you. You can take it off."

Law of Intention: One Day at a Time

They circled back toward the bench where they had started. The sky was fully awake now, and the jogger they'd seen earlier passed them again on his second lap.

Cornelius sat slowly, with more effort than Marius remembered him needing before. A brief flicker crossed the old man's face, as if his body had betrayed him for just a moment, but he smoothed it away.

"Marius," he said, "do you remember the first law I taught you?"

Marius nodded. "Shorten the day."

"And now," Cornelius said, "you must learn to shape the day."

He took out the well-used notebook he often carried and placed it on Marius's lap.

"At the beginning," he said, "you needed only one rescue: to stop carrying years at once. Now you must master something more subtle: to stop living everyone else's day at once."

He drew a line on the page and wrote, in his careful, deliberate hand:

The Law of Intention

A day ruled by the Clock exhausts you.

A day ruled by the Compass completes you.

He slid the notebook back toward Marius.

"A day ruled by the Clock," he said, "leaves you scattered - busy but not fruitful, connected but not present, active but not alive."

"A day ruled by the Compass," he went on, "may be full, even tiring, but at the end of it, there is a strange satisfaction. Your body may ache, but your soul is at peace."

Marius reread the words.

"So how do I do it?" he asked. "In one ordinary day, with all its interruptions and noise - how do I live by the Compass, not the Clock?"

For the first time that morning, a delicate smile caught at the corner of Cornelius's mouth.

"You already know," he said. "You just need a ritual."

The Daily Victory - Mirror Before Window

Cornelius leaned back, eyes on the sky as if reading something written there.

"Here is what you will do," he said. "And you will not treat it as a suggestion. You will treat it as survival."

Marius straightened again at the mood.

"Before you look at a screen," Cornelius said, "before you check a message, before you open the window of the world, you will sit in silence for three minutes."

"Three?" Marius said. "That's all?"

Cornelius nodded. "If you cannot give three minutes to intention, you are already owned by the Clock."

He held up a hand.

"In those three minutes, you will do four things."

He began to count them off.

"First: Breathe."

"Slowly. Deeply. Let your body remember it is not in a war zone."

"Second: Give thanks."

"Name three things, no matter how small, for which you are grateful. This clears the fog from the mirror."

"Third: Name your one intention."

Take thirty seconds now; write yours. Let this be a short pause to reflect and set your heart and mind on a single, clear purpose. Consider what one intention will guide you today, regardless of the noise around you or the demands weighing on you.

"Fourth: Ask for help."

"Whisper it if you must. 'Teach me to number this day. Guard my heart from hurry. Let me walk it, not chase it.'"

He lowered his hand.

"Then," he said, "and only then, may you open the window."

Marius let the steps soak in. They sounded simple. Almost too simple.

Cornelius appeared to perceive the skepticism.

"You are thinking," he said, "'How could three minutes change my life?'"

Marius gave a sheepish half-smile. "Something like that."

Cornelius's eyes sharpened again.

"Those three minutes," he said, "are not for changing your life. They are for changing your posture toward it. A man who enters his day with a bowed head and a clear intention stands differently, speaks differently, chooses differently."

He paused.

"Intention," he added, "is the spine of the day. Without it, the hours slump under the weight of other people's expectations." He paused and then asked, "Why does this intention matter to you, Marius? What purpose does it serve in your life?" Marius considered the question, realizing that linking his intentions into a more profound 'why' would not only clarify his actions but additionally strengthen his firmness to carry them out. Identifying the core purpose of each intention, he turned mere tasks into meaningful pursuits, coordinating his day with a direction that rang deeply on a personal level.

If you find pieces of yourself in Marius - always behind, always rushing, constantly measuring your ordinary hours against someone else's highlight reel - then this is your invitation too.

You do not need another productivity system.

You need a new way to begin.

Tonight, set a small card by your bed, or a note on your nightstand, with these words:

Mirror Before Window.

Who am I turning into?

What is most important today?

What is my one intention?

And tomorrow, when your eyes open and your hand reaches reflexively for the nearest device, let the card interrupt you.

Take your three minutes. Breathe. Give thanks. Set one intention. Ask quietly for help. What usually steals your first three minutes? Consider the interruptions or routines that may interfere with your intention-setting. Identifying these hindrances can be the first step toward assuring your day begins with deliberate focus.

You will not win every day. Some mornings you will forget. Some days, the Clock will shout louder than the Compass. It is completely normal to miss a day or struggle to find your balance.

At such times, it's important to offer yourself grace and patience. Remember, resilience is built through your willingness to restart. Whenever you stumble, gently remind yourself that every new day offers an opportunity to begin again without guilt, helping you cultivate self-compassion as you continue moving forward.

If you practice this ritual for seven days, then fourteen, then thirty, you will feel something begin to shift. As you continue, you may find your reactions slowing down. Your anger takes a few steps back. Comparison begins to lose its sharpest teeth.

For people managing unpredictable or hectic mornings, consider adapting this practice to fit your rhythm. You might use moments of quiet during your daily travel, or take comfort in a few mindful minutes at lunch. Remember, the heart of intention is not bound to the confines of time but strives to be present within it.

Your hours, even if flawed, can seem less like a blur and more like a series of chosen moments. You will discover that a day is not too long when it is aimed in one true direction.

The Silent Exigency of a Final Lesson

Back on the bench, the park had fully awakened.

Children's voices floated from a playground nearby. Dogs tugged their owners along the paths. Cars hummed past the trees.

Marius shut the notebook gently.

"So," he said, "I don't need to live faster."

Cornelius shook his head.

"You need to live truer," he said. "Depth over speed. Direction over motion. Compass over Clock."

Marius looked at him, really looked, noticing the slight pallor in his skin, the way he pressed his hand briefly to his chest when he shifted, as if steadying something inside.

"Why are you… So intense about this one?" Marius asked.

Cornelius's eyes wandered toward the horizon, where the sun was climbing, slow and certain.

"Because," he said in a low voice, "direction is the last lesson."

He turned back, for a momentary pause; there seemed to be a nearly fierce look in his eyes.

"I have seen men survive grief," he said. "I have watched them endure failure, crawl through shame, rebuild after ruin, only to lose themselves in success, in hurry, in comparison."

He leaned forward, his cane resting between both hands.

"If you do not master intention," he said, each word deliberate, "the very life you are building will one day devour you."

The sentence sat among them like a stone.

Marius swallowed.

"I don't want that," he said. "I don't want to arrive somewhere I never chose, just because I was moving too fast to notice."

Cornelius's features softened again. The flash of fire in his eyes tapered back into the tender steadiness Marius knew so well.

"Then begin tomorrow differently," he said. "And when you forget tomorrow, begin the day after that. This is not perfection. It is practice."

He rose slowly to his feet.

"Do not let the world's hurry steal your heart," he added, voice subdued though unwavering. "It will take your joy next. Master your pauses, and you master your path."

Marius stood too.

"Will you…see me again tomorrow?" he asked.

Cornelius smiled, a small, quiet smile that carried both tenderness and something Marius couldn't name.

"If the Author grants me another page," he said, "I will gladly walk through it with you."

He reached out, squeezed Marius's shoulder, just once, firmly, and began to walk down the path, his figure framed by the growing light.

Marius watched him go, an unease stirring in his chest that he couldn't explain.

He sat back down on the bench and took out his notebook.

On a fresh page, he wrote in slow, clear letters:

Mirror before the window.

Compass before clock.

One intention.

One day.

He closed the book and let the daybreak illumination rest on his face.

For the first time in a long time, he did not feel rushed.

The city moved around him - cars rushing, feet pounding, phones buzzing - but inside, something had finally grown still.

A day, he realized, is not too long when it is lived with a single, chosen direction.

He rose from the bench, not quickly, not slowly, but deliberately.

The next day would come.

So would the noise.

So would the demands.

But tomorrow, he would greet it differently.

Not with panic.

With intention.

And somewhere, just past the boundary of his awareness, another kind of day was drawing near - a day when Cornelius would no longer sit beside him on park benches…

…but the Compass he had given would remain.

Chapter Twelve: The Final Lesson - Perspective and the "Why Me?" Syndrome

"A man's days are his life in miniature. What he does with one, he will do with all."

— Cornelius.

"Circumstances do not make the man; they reveal him to himself."

— James Allen.

"Let us rejoice while in tribulations, since we know that tribulation produces endurance."

— Romans 5:3

The Morning That Changed Everything

The world was still when Marius opened his eyes - a thin hush before dawn, when time feels tender, and the air holds its sigh. For a long moment, he lay listening to the peace, the slight chiming of the clock, the soft pace of his own breathing. There was no urgency in that hour, no alarm sounding him into motion. Only quiet, and in that hush, a decision waiting to be born.

He rose slowly, as though moving through sacred ground. The window was pale with the first trace of sunrise glow. On the small table sat his well-used notebook, its corners bent, its pages scarred with half-written plans, abandoned goals, and fragments of self-promises left unmet.

He sat down, pen grasped, and waited for thought to find form.

In the soft radiance of the lamp, he remembered Cornelius's voice, calm and solid as ever:

"The secret of a fulfilled life is not hidden in grand plans, Marius, but in ordinary hours, lived deliberately."

The words vibrated through him with new weight.

He realized how much of his life had been spent pursuing the distant sky - always running toward someday, always postponing peace. He had measured his worth by unfinished dreams, his joy by distant outcomes. Yet Cornelius had been right all along. The measure of a life was not in the years ahead, but in the single sunrise that could be commanded, called today.

Marius turned to a blank page. The paper radiated dimly in the daybreak glow, as if waiting for purpose. For the first time in many years, his question changed. No longer, what should I do with my life? But what shall I do with this day?

That thought occurred less significant - yet infinitely more powerful.

He drew a slow breath, wrote the date at the top of the page, and underlined it once, firmly. Then, with the surety of a man who had uncovered once more his footing, he wrote a single line:

Today will count.

The simplicity of those words bore the strain of a vow. Something in him moved - not with fireworks or fanfare, yet surrounded by the quiet gravity of truth finally understood. The storms that formerly drove him no longer frightened him. The failures that had troubled him stopped defining him. Each one had been a teacher pointing to this very morning.

For Marius, the day no longer appeared as a burden to survive. It served as a clean sheet to paint, a seed to tend, a sacred space to build meaning within. He finally understood what Cornelius had meant when he said,

"A day is too long only when it has no purpose."

He closed his eyes, and briefly, the image of Cornelius came alive in his mind - the old man's smile, the shine in his eyes, the tenderness in the sound of his words. Marius could faintly hear him say, "You have learned the law of correction, my boy. Now learn the discipline of direction."

He looked toward the rising light outside the window. The initial rays brushed across the rooftops, and the city stirred awake. But this morning, Marius felt no hurry to join the noise. The world would move fast enough; he would move with purpose.

He reached for his cup of coffee and offered a slight smile. It was neither strong nor perfect, but it was his.

For the first time in a long while, he felt the power that comes from stillness - a courage that did not roar but whispered.

He realized now that a man's life is not built in decades or destinies - it is built in days. And each day, if lived with intention, becomes a quiet victory that no storm can undo.

That morning, Marius began again.

He began not to conquer the world, but to master a single sunrise.

He began not by erasing his past, but by redeeming his present.

He began to live - deliberately, gratefully, and awake.

And though he did not yet know it, that one line he had written - Today will count - would become the compass by which he would steer every morning that followed.

The Law of the Day

Cornelius had many sayings, but the one that inscribed itself deepest into Marius's mind was this:

"The unit of destiny is the day."

He repeated it often, not as a mantra, yet as a cue, a gentle correction every time Marius drifted into the fog of tomorrow.

"Years, he explained, confuse the human spirit. They softly utter assurances of endless chances and tell a man he has time to spare. Years tempt a person to postpone life until a better season arrives.

But the day never lies.

A sunrise gives you a beginning.

A sunset closes the page.

A day, Cornelius said, is honest - too honest to let you hide."

Marius realized that every single day was like a clean slate before him. He represented more than an observer of its unfolding; he was an active author, forming its tale.

"What sentence will you write to open your day?" Cornelius would often ask, instilling a powerful consciousness of responsibility and privilege in self-authorship. Marius understood that the meaning of a day is not bestowed upon it but created through his actions, thoughts, and intentions.

A calm morning in the past, as daylight crept slowly into Marius's small kitchen, he had finally grasped what Cornelius meant. He had spent much of his life trying to manage entire years at once, bearing the burden of next week, next month, the next ten years. No wonder each day had felt like a load. He was hauling futures that had not yet been born.

Cornelius had tried to warn him, quoting a line from the Master's own teaching:

"So never be anxious about the next day, for the next day will have its own anxieties. Each day has enough of its own troubles." **— Matthew 6:34**

Cornelius had explained it simply:

"When you drag tomorrow into today, you double the load and half the strength."

The message had struck Marius deeply. The wisdom was ancient, but the consolation was immediate. He had been exhausting himself not by what the day demanded, but by what tomorrow threatened. He was fighting shadows that never touched him.

He remembered one afternoon when Cornelius leaned back on the wooden bench in the park beside him and said quietly:

"Do you wish to change your life, Marius? Then master one day. Treat the next daybreak as a gift, not a guarantee."

Those words remodeled the very architecture of Marius's thinking.

He started to realize that a day is a manageable miracle. Not a year. Not a decade. Not the entire direction of his life. Just twenty-four hours. A single thread from the pattern of eternity - enough to focus on, enough to influence, enough to change.

Cornelius often compared it to carving stone.

"No sculptor shapes the entire statue at once. He chips away one section at a time. If he rushed to carve the whole at once, he would ruin everything."

Life, he had insisted, works the same way.

Marius learned to live by that law.

Each morning, he asked himself one question:

"What is the one thing I can do today that honors the breath in my lungs?"

Just one thing. One act. One focus. One deliberate choice.

He discovered peace in that simplicity. The confusion inside his mind quieted. The burden on his shoulders lightened. The day came across less like a mountain and more like a path, one step, then another.

Cornelius's voice often repeated in his mind as the day developed:

"Master the day, Marius. Master just this one day, and the years will bow in respect."

Marius discovered that change doesn't happen in revolutions but in repetitions. A well-lived day is a seed. Plant enough of them, and you grow a forest.

Every night, before extinguishing the bedside lamp, he now spoke quietly:

"Today mattered."

At times, days were victories. Others were simply steps. But each one was lived completely, honestly, with intention.

And as he lay his head down, he finally understood another truth Cornelius had hinted at many times:

"A day is not too long - when it is lived with purpose."

"A day becomes too long only when you try to carry the next one on your back."

Perspective: The Hidden Engine of Intention

Now, sitting in the dimming light of another evening, Marius found himself in the same urban garden where he and Cornelius had talked long toward the twilight. The bench was the same. The jasmine vines still perfumed the air. But Cornelius was not beside him.

Instead, his words were.

Marius broke the quietude with a hushed tone meant only for the past and for himself.

"I understand the importance of purpose," he spoke gently, remembering his own voice on that earlier night. "I've been trying to live with intention, to do each day on purpose. But some mornings still feel heavy before I even rise from bed. No matter how focused I try to be, the weight returns. Why me, Cornelius?"

He could still see the old man turning toward him in memory, his countenance easing with recognition.

"Ah," Cornelius had spoken in a gentle tone, "the oldest question on earth."

In Marius's mind, the scene replayed with perfect clarity. Cornelius reached down and picked up two stones lying at the edge of the walkway. He placed them resting in his palm: one smooth as polished marble, the other sharp and uneven like a piece of broken pavement.

"They came from the same soil," Cornelius had said, rolling them lightly between his fingers. "Felt the same storms. Carried the same history."

He held up the smooth one.

"This stone trusted the river. It let the current shape it."

Then he raised the rough one.

"This one hid. It feared movement. The water passed around it, but never over it. No shaping. No smoothing. Only resistance."

Even now, Marius could feel that calm stare on him, though Cornelius wasn't with him, but he could hear him say:

"The storm rarely decides a man's shape. His perspective does."

Those words reached Marius again with the equal calm force of truth. He realized how long he had lived assuming that circumstances shape people - but here, in two small stones that he still kept in a drawer at home, lay the evidence that outlook has far more power than experience.

He remembered how Cornelius had placed the stones into his hands.

"When you ask, 'Why me?' your gaze drops backward. The spirit freezes. The heart waits for rescue. But when a man asks, 'What now?' the road appears under his feet. That question turns pain into direction."

A breeze moved amid the leaves overhead now, just as it had then. Somewhere in the distance, a cyclist passed. A child's laughter wafted in the air. The city remained breathing, as though the time had folded back on itself.

In his mind, Cornelius's voice had gone on with a story that glowed with life.

"There was a blind beggar named Bartimaeus," he'd said. "He sat on a roadside much like this one. Many walked past him without noticing him. But when he heard that hope was near, he cried out, 'Jesus, Son of David, have mercy on me!' People tried to silence him, yet he called louder. His eyes were dark, but his vision was clear **(Mark 10:46-52)."**

Cornelius had given a quiet smile.

"Bartimaeus' intention wasn't simply to see the world - he intended to see possibility. He recognized the One who could change the course of his life. His focus was sharper than his sight."

Even now, Marius carried the heaviness of that story inside him. Bartimaeus's cry was not the cry of a victim. It was the voice of a man who had decided to see before his eyes opened, which was why Jesus said to him, "Your faith has made you well."

Marius could nearly sense the old familiar pressure of Cornelius's hand on his shoulder.

"Intention begins long before action," Cornelius had said. "Intention lives inside perspective - the way a man frames the world before the world speaks back. A clear perspective fuels every purposeful step. A distorted one keeps a man walking in circles."

Sitting alone on the bench now, Marius lifted his eyes to the moving sky - the way Cornelius had done.

"When perspective changes," he heard again, "despair becomes instruction. Problems become pathways. Obstacles become material for growth. A man who sees through the lens of possibility moves differently - he rises earlier, thinks sharper, endures longer. Perspective is the unseen force that shapes every choice."

Marius slipped a hand into his pocket and touched one smooth stone he had begun carrying there.

"Carry this," Cornelius had told him that night. "Let it remind you that shaping takes place in motion, not in hiding."

The urban lights gleamed to full brightness around him now. Night settled, not with heaviness, but with the feeling of a curtain drawing open to reveal a new stage.

He rose slowly from the bench, feeling unburdened though nothing external had changed. The load on his chest had not vanished, yet the angle of his sight had. He ceased to feel pressed beneath life - he felt positioned within it.

At every step homeward, he tasted again that first hint of clarity that had come when he dared to look differently at the same road.

And he understood once more, without needing the lesson repeated:

When a man chooses his perspective, he chooses his direction.

When his direction shifts, his life follows.

Perspective is the hidden engine of intention, the quiet force that turns the ordinary day into the path of purpose.

The Mirror and the Window

Back in his apartment, with the city thriving below, Marius stood opposite the small bathroom mirror and watched his own reflection breathe. Behind the glass, he perceived beyond his face, but years of conversations with Cornelius layered like transparencies over the image.

Cornelius had often reminded him that a man lives his entire life through two viewpoints - the mirror and the window.

"We have spoken of windows before," he previously had said, "of how perception shapes the world you see. But there is a deeper glass - the mirror."

Marius could still see him tapping two fingers against his chest.

"The mirror reveals the inner world - the thoughts you permit, the beliefs you carry, the conversations you hold with yourself when no one else can hear. And the window reveals the outer world. But here is the secret: When the mirror is fogged, the window is lied to."

He remembered asking what he meant.

In his mind's eye, Cornelius pointed toward a nearby window, its glass blurred by morning condensation.

"Look. That window hasn't changed the world outside - it only hides it. When a man's spirit fogs - when his internal mirror is dirty with self-doubt - he sees the world as smaller than it is. He projects his own smudge onto the landscape."

Marius could almost feel that tender hand on his shoulder again.

"Most people start their morning with a fogged mirror - criticizing themselves before their feet hit the floor - and then wonder why the view out the window looks so hopeless."

Those words had settled into him long ago, and now, alone before the mirror, they rose again with new clarity. He realized how many mornings he had walked into the world with a mind clouded by complaint, disappointment, and fear - and how those inner storms had molded everything he saw around him.

He heard Cornelius's voice continue in memory:

"When a man wakes up rehearsing what hurts, the day bends under the weight of his own voice. But when he polishes the mirror with gratitude, even a small kind - the day shifts. The world has not changed, yet everything looks different."

Marius had witnessed it himself. On days when he woke discouraged, the city appeared cold, people unkind, and challenges overwhelming. On days when he woke with even a slight trace of thankfulness - a memory, a blessing, a modest recognition of breath and possibility - the same city appeared lively, the same problems manageable, the same world welcoming.

He uttered softly to his reflection now, as if reciting a law, he finally accepted:

"The mirror determines the window."

A man never sees the world as it truly is; he sees it as he is.

He remembered the mornings he had looked into the mirror, his heart flooded with worry, and the rest of the day ahead seemed crowded with shadows. Every inconvenience seemed personal, each postponement felt like a danger, and even the simplest tasks felt cumbersome. The mirror of his inner life - smeared with doubt, fear, and self-criticism - colored everything he had seen outside the window.

And yet, he also remembered the mornings when the mirror was polished - even lightly. A clean mirror had reflected a more courageous self, a steadier will, a quieter confidence. Through that clearer mirror, the outside world had taken on a new shape. Problems had looked solvable. People had seemed kinder, and the day itself had seemed less like a burden and more like a path.

"Clear the mirror, and the window clears with it," Cornelius had formerly summarized.

Marius let that sentence sit in his chest, resembling a stone of calm.

He saw now that external battles were often traces of internal ones.

The world hadn't grown darker - his thoughts had.

The world hadn't grown colder - his heart had chilled.

The world hadn't conspired against him - his own interpretation had toughened.

As his viewpoint changed, he started to perceive the hidden architecture of his days:

A worried mirror creates anxious windows.

A grateful mirror creates generous windows.

A hopeful mirror reveals open paths where hopeless eyes see dead ends.

A renewed mirror makes typical days brighter, more precise, shorter, and purposeful.

"If you wish to change your day," he heard Cornelius say again inside his memory, "begin with the mirror.

If you wish to change your life, begin with the mirror repeatedly."

Because a man cannot see possibilities through a window clouded by his personal despair.

He cannot recognize blessings when his own reflection calls him unworthy.

He cannot walk toward purpose if his inner sight has gone dim.

"The world responds to the man who sees himself clearly," Cornelius had added once.

Marius gave a slow nod to his own reflection.

He grasped now: the mirror - the inner beliefs, the mindset, the posture of the heart - quietly scripts the view through every window he will ever look through.

A day can feel unbearably long, not because the hours extend without end, but because a fogged mirror makes each hour more burdensome than before.

He drew a thumb across the glass, as if wiping away invisible mist.

"Clear the mirror," he uttered gently, "and the day shortens.

Clear the mirror, and the world widens.

Clear the mirror, and life itself begins again."

He heard Cornelius's final summary in his mind:

"The man who cannot command his perspective cannot command his day.

Living intentionally does not begin with schedules or goals. It starts with sight - inward sight and outward sight. A polished mind meets a clearer world."

Marius turned off the bathroom light with a softer heart. Every morning, he now knew, would offer him that same choice: which mirror to polish, which window to open.

The day would not shrink or stretch.

But his perspective would.

Defining Intention

At the small kitchen table, with his notebook open and the words Today will count still fresh on the page, Marius thought back to another walk by the river - one of the many times when Cornelius had turned an ordinary path into a classroom.

Cornelius had told him then that a man's life changes long before his circumstances ever do.

"Every transformation begins," he had said, "on the morning a man decides who he intends to be."

Marius remembered how people had streamed past them that day as if pushed by an invisible wind, from task to task, emotion to emotion, problem to problem - living exactly as Cornelius described: drifting.

"They wake up waiting for the world to announce the kind of day it will be," Cornelius had said. "And so, the world decides for them."

But intention, he'd explained, worked differently.

Intention is the inner commander.

Intention is the quiet architect that shapes a day before it even begins.

Cornelius had called it the invisible steering wheel - not the loud energy of motivation, but the still, deliberate strength of direction.

"A man without intention," he'd said, "moves like a ship without a captain. He floats, but he never arrives."

Marius remembered, at that instant, confessing that he was habituated to feeling lost even when he was busy.

Cornelius had laughed quietly.

"Activity is not arrival, my boy. You can run in circles all day and never travel an inch. Intention turns movement into progress."

They had stopped at the railing overlooking the river, the metropolitan lights glimmering across the water like dispersed coins.

"Before the sun rises," Cornelius had told him, "Ask yourself one question:

Who will I be today?

Not what I will accomplish - that is secondary. First, decide the character you will bring into the hours ahead. The day will obey the man who commands himself."

To bring the lesson home, Cornelius had told him the story of Daniel - taken from his home, placed under pressure, surrounded by people and customs far different from his faith. Yet Daniel had prospered because "he resolved in his heart" before the test ever came. His intention preceded his trial, and because of it, he stood where others fell.

"Life does not honor talent first," Cornelius had said then. "Life honors direction."

Now, at his quiet table, Marius saw the truth of it more clearly than ever.

Intention was not wishful thinking. It was a conscious, disciplined declaration:

This is who I choose to be, no matter what the day holds.

That choice determined everything.

He had lived without intention once and knew its price: becoming vulnerable to every emotion, every interruption, and all fears. But with intention, he had begun to feel anchored - not unshakable, but steady enough to regain his balance quickly.

Intention did not ignore reality; it simply refused to be ruled by it.

"Drifting is natural. Directing is chosen," he heard Cornelius say in memory. "One is a habit; the other is a power."

Marius lifted his pen and wrote on the page beneath his vow for the day:

Who will I be today?

He paused, then answered in simple, deliberate words - not for the world, but for his own soul.

The difference between a wasted day and a purposeful one, he now knew, began in that first silent pause - before the world entered, before the demands rose, before the noise flooded in.

Intention was the key that unlocked the day.

And once unlocked, a single day could begin to reshape an entire life.

The Law of Dual Vision

Later, as the darkness advanced and shadows darkened across his living room floor, Marius reached into a bowl on the shelf and closed his hand around two familiar pebbles.

They were the same stones Cornelius once had rolled in his hand by the river.

He remembered that night clearly. The river had caught the last glints of softening light, and a load had pressed into Marius's chest. The events of those weeks had stretched him thin - too thin - and he had admitted in a faint utterance, "Sometimes my heart beats so hard from worry that I feel drained before the day even begins. My strength feels gone. Even the light in my eyes feels dim."

Cornelius had listened quietly, nodding with an understanding calm.

"Many great men," he had softly said, "have reached the same moment. David once confessed that his heart hammered within him, strength drained, and the light in his eyes flickered away. He was not weak - he was human."

Then Cornelius picked up two small pebbles from the ground, rolled them, and allowed them to rest in his right palm.

"These stones came from the same river," he'd said. "The same rain, the same storms, the same floods touched them both. One is smooth. The other is jagged. The difference is simple: one allowed the current to shape it, the other tried to hide from the water."

He had placed both stones in Marius's hand.

"This lesson," Cornelius said, "is the law of dual vision. Every event in a man's life carries two possible meanings: one seen from the ground, and the other seen from higher ground."

Marius had frowned. "So, I'm supposed to pretend the pain doesn't sting?"

"No," Cornelius had answered. "Pain is real. Exhaustion is real. Your pounding heart and dimmed vision are not signs of failure. They are signs that life has pressed you hard enough to awaken something deeper. Pain is never the teacher - but pain often opens the classroom door."

To help him see it, Cornelius had reminded him of Joseph - betrayed by his own brothers, sold into slavery, imprisoned for a crime fabricated by another, forgotten for years.

"From the ground," he'd said, "Joseph saw heartbreak. But when he rose in perspective, he saw a pattern. He later told his brothers, 'You meant harm, but God shaped it toward good.' Joseph learned to rise high enough to see purpose where others only saw pain."

Cornelius had slanted his head then, studying Marius's tired expression.

"You are looking at your life from the valley," he'd said. "Everything feels bigger down there. Problems look like giants, and hope looks like a rumor. But lift your eyes - even a little - and the whole landscape changes."

To make the lesson more straightforward, he'd narrated a story from the neighborhood:

"There's a woman who runs the flower shop on Seventh Street," he'd said. "When she was laid off from her corporate job, she sat in her car and wept until she couldn't see straight. Her heart pounded. Her strength drained. Her vision blurred - just like David's. But losing that job forced her to pick up the dream she had buried for ten years. Now look at her store - bouquets, colors, joy. She told me that the worst week of her life carried her to the doorway of her best one."

"Your trial may become the doorway to your best life ever,' Cornelius had mused, "if you are intentional."

Cornelius had smiled tenderly.

"Two meanings. One from fear. One from higher ground."

Bending nearer, he'd added:

"You cannot control the event. But you can choose your elevation. When a man rises in thought, he rises in strength. When he rises in strength, his eyes recover their light."

Now, standing alone in his apartment, Marius closed his fingers around the two stones once more.

Purpose did not demand a life free from weariness.

It simply asked that he rise high enough to see what his exhaustion was trying to teach him.

"A day is too long," he uttered, recalling Cornelius's conclusion, "for the man who lives it from the ground. But the day becomes manageable - even meaningful - for the man who rises high enough to interpret it."

The Lost Art of Beginning the Day

The next morning, Marius woke before his alarm, the room still shadowed by pre-dawn gray. The stack of bills on the counter remained. The unfinished assignments at work remained. The uncertainty about his future persisted.

But now, he understood that something else remained, too: choice.

He remembered how, after learning the Law of Dual Vision, he had previously said to Cornelius, "I wake up already tired - as if the day has decided itself before I even open my eyes."

Cornelius's reply had been simple:

"A man rises or falls with the first thought he greets the morning with."

Back then, Marius had passed it off as an old man's proverb. Now, sitting again at his kitchen table with dawn slowly brushing color onto the world, he understood.

If perspective was the engine of intention, the morning was the ignition.

A day left to impulse would always run wild.

A day claimed early would walk in obedience.

Cornelius had called it the lost art of beginning the day - lost, because most people no longer rose with purpose. They rose with panic.

"They don't wake up and greet the day," he had said once. "They wake up and fight it. They check their phones before they check their spirits. They rush into hours they haven't anchored. They react long before they reflect."

"An unclaimed morning," he had warned, "will soon become an unruly day."

To show him why, Cornelius had recounted the story of a brilliant designer whose life always felt disorganized, frantic, and unfinished. The man had talent, but his mornings controlled him. If he woke late, the day collapsed. If he received an unexpected message that arrived early, the day unraveled. His entire life bent under the burden of mornings he never commanded.

"And yet," Cornelius had added, "when the man decided to rise fifteen minutes earlier each day simply to breathe, pray, and think - not to rush - everything began to align. Not because life changed, but because he did."

Inspired by that long-ago conversation, Marius now opened his notebook to a fresh page, creating the framework for The Alignment Ritual, a grounding practice learned from Cornelius. This ritual consisted of three small guiding questions, written before anything else:

1. What matters most today?
2. Who can I help today?
3. What must I finish, no matter what?

To smoothly incorporate this ritual into his morning routine, Marius chose a moment he would encounter every day: the time spent waiting for his coffee to brew. By coordinating this self-examining practice with an existing habit, he found it easier to embrace and sustain, and the questions calmed him. They offered his thoughts direction and his heart a consistent beat.

The first time he had done this, months ago, he had felt foolish, as though a few lines on paper could shift the view of his life. But each time, the questions calmed him. They gave his thoughts direction and his heart a regular tempo.

"Focus is a boundary. Purpose is a compass," Cornelius had told him. "When you begin with both, the day cannot scatter you."

Marius thought of another lesson Cornelius had pointed him to, the quiet habit of Jesus before dawn.

Mark had recorded that Jesus woke early, while it was still dark, and withdrew to pray. Not because He was weak, Cornelius had explained, but because intention requires solitude. Strength demands silence. Clarity needs space before responsibility begins.

"Divine wisdom," Cornelius had said, "begins in stillness, not in the noise of a rushing morning."

Marius felt that truth more deeply now than ever. His mornings had formerly belonged to stress, dread, and uncompleted tasks. Now they belonged to the direction.

He remembered walking once beneath budding trees while Cornelius said:

"Most men hope the day will be kind. The wise man makes the day kind by anchoring his first hour."

Beginning the day deliberately, Cornelius had explained, was like building the base of a house. A weak foundation invited collapse; a strong one invited stability.

"A man who commands the morning," he had said, "commands the momentum."

So, Marius took a breath and answered his three questions slowly.

A day was too long for the man who entered it unprepared.

But it became manageable, even meaningful, when entered with ritual and intention.

He shut the notebook and felt, not ready for everything yet, but in sync with something, and that was enough.

The Compass and the Clock

On his way to work, Marius passed the hill where he and Cornelius had previously sat overlooking the city, the same wooden bench where their path had first intertwined. He didn't climb up that morning, but the memory climbed to meet him.

He could still see Cornelius drawing two circles in the dirt with a small stick.

"This," the old man had said, tapping the first circle, "is the clock, the measure of your hours, the count of your minutes, the structure of your day."

He had tapped the second circle.

"And this is the compass, the meaning behind those hours, the direction behind those minutes, the purpose steering the day."

The breeze had brushed their faces while the city rushed and tangled below.

"Most people," Cornelius had said, "live only in the first circle. They chase minutes but never meaning. They rush because the clock is loud, but the compass is quiet."

Marius knew that life all too well - a calendar full of obligations, a mind full of deadlines, a heart running on empty. His days had felt unbearably long because he had been serving the wrong master: the relentless clock, not the purposeful compass.

"Time is a servant. Purpose is the master," Cornelius had said steadily. "When the order reverses, life becomes a confusion."

To illustrate, he had told Marius about a gifted chef who worked fourteen-hour shifts, driven and ambitious but drained by the pace. She had measured her success minute by minute, task by task, until exhaustion nearly broke her. One day, after collapsing into a chair between orders, she'd finally asked herself:

"Why am I giving so much time to this?"

That single question awakened her compass. She realized her true passion wasn't grinding out meals but teaching others the art she loved. When purpose became her guide, her schedule fell into place. She worked fewer hours, but lived fuller days.

"She didn't change careers," Cornelius had said. "She changed direction."

"A day grows heavy when the clock leads," he had added. "A day grows holy when the compass leads."

Cornelius had then opened his well-used notebook and read aloud:

"Teach us how to count our days, so that we may acquire a heart of wisdom." **— Psalm 90:12**

He had shut the notebook gently.

"That scripture does not speak of counting days as a miser counts coins," he'd explained. "It speaks of weighing days - asking what they are worth, not merely how they pass."

Marius remembered asking, "How do I know if I'm living by the clock or by the compass?"

Cornelius's smile had been small but piercing.

"Look at your exhaustion," he'd replied. "If you are tired in the body, you worked hard.

If you are tired in the soul, you worked without meaning."

"A day directed by purpose becomes lighter, even if busy," he had said. "A day without purpose becomes heavy, even if idle."

Now, as Marius walked through the morning traffic, he heard that distinction again and bore the heaviness shifting inside him. He had devoted years to counting minutes and missing meaning. No wonder his days had previously felt unbearably long.

"When the clock and the compass walk together," he could still hear Cornelius say, "the day becomes a masterpiece."

That night, Marius would once again write in his journal:

"Time becomes a burden when I try to carry it.

Time becomes a blessing when I give it direction."

And he would remember that a day is too long only when lived without purpose, but when led by a compass of clear intention, a day becomes just enough to change everything.

The Discipline of the Pause

The following week, after a string of demanding days, Marius entered quietly the same small café where he and Cornelius had regularly shared a quiet table by the window. The morning rush was over; a few customers persisted in a cushion of soft conversation and steam.

Cornelius was not there now, yet the recollection of those earlier visits slipped into the chair across from him like a loving father.

He remembered a particular day, the restlessness he had carried then - the same knot of wires in his chest that beat and throbbed, refusing to be neatly untangled. Life had been demanding too much, too fast, all at once.

Cornelius had noticed without being told.

"The strength of a man," he had expressed softly, stirring his coffee once, "is measured in his stillness long before anyone sees his stride."

Before Marius could have answered, a man at the counter had suddenly shouted in anger, shouting at the café attendant for mixing up his drink wrongly. The young barista had apologized, offered to correct the error, but the man had snapped again and stormed out, leaving bitterness behind like haze drifting in his wake.

Cornelius had watched quietly, then turned back to Marius.

"Did you see? The clock rules that man, not the compass."

Marius had frowned. "You mean he was in a hurry?"

Cornelius had shaken his head. "No. He was in a habit. A man who reacts without pausing shows plainly who governs him - impulse or intention."

He had tapped his spoon tenderly against the cup.

"Pause before you react. That pause is the hinge on which the entire day turns."

He had gone on to explain that every reaction carries a sacred second - a moment so small that most people never notice it. A second in which instinct pulls intensely in one direction, yet wisdom waits quietly in the other.

"Many storms in a man's life," he had said, "are born in that single, unguarded second."

An insult lands, and instinct demands retaliation.

A fear rises, and instinct urges retreat.

A setback stings, and instinct whispers defeat.

A temptation calls, and instinct invites surrender.

"But if you pause - even for one breath - you return to command," Cornelius had said, lifting a finger. "A pause never signals weakness. A pause signals mastery."

He had leaned back, thoughtful.

"David understood this well - the shepherd who walked amid struggles, betrayal, and heartbreak. In one of his darkest confessions, he wrote:

'My heart pounds, my strength fails, and the light of my eyes has left me.'— **Psalm 38:10**

"A coward did not speak those words," Cornelius had whispered, "but by a king who paused - because clarity was needed before the next step."

He had closed the café's leather menu with a quiet finality.

"Even the strongest men pause."

Then Cornelius had told him the story of a choking executive whose mentor gave him just one instruction:

"Every time the elevator door closes, pause."

Each morning, as those doors glided shut, the man had inhaled, exhaled, and allowed intention - not panic - to guide the next floor. That tiny pause - just one breath - had modified him. His temper softened. His clarity sharpened. His leadership strengthened.

"A day is too long for a man who reacts," Cornelius had concluded. "A day becomes manageable for a man who pauses."

Sitting in the same café now, Marius closed his eyes for a breath and practiced what he'd been taught.

He remembered days when a single irritation had ruined hours afterward - not because the irritation was powerful, but because he had never paused long enough to reclaim the day.

"Every pause is a crossroads," Cornelius had said. "One road leads to regret. The other leads to mastery."

In the ensuing days, Marius had applied the discipline:

A driver cut him off - he paused.

His boss sent a terse email - he paused.

Old fears whispered - he paused.

Temptation from his past prodded at him - he paused.

And with each moment of stillness, his strength had returned before his reaction escaped.

Now, as he finished his coffee alone, he uttered to himself,

"No man can command an entire day. The weight crushes him. But every man can command a single pause. And that pause commands the next step."

He moved out into the bright mid-morning light - a world still loud, still hurried, still demanding. But it no longer intimidated him.

He held alongside him the one tool that might change even the longest of days…one sacred pause at a time.

The Parable of the Clockmaker

On an afternoon when the sky draped low and gray over the city, Marius found himself meandering into an older quarter, his feet tracing the route his memory already knew.

He stopped outside a familiar shop whose windows glowed with warm, amber light. The notice above the door displayed:

The Clocksmith's Hand - Repairs & Restorations.

He did not go this time. He didn't need to. The moment he saw the lettering, the entire visit with Cornelius played out in his mind.

He remembered stepping inside to the quiet buzz of countless ticking clocks. Brass, wood, silver, and glass - each face furrowed with its own tempo, each pendulum swaying like a rhythmic beat that declined to hurry.

Behind an aged wooden bench had sat an elderly clockmaker, silver-haired and steady-handed, leaning over a delicate pocket watch. His movements had been slow, precise, reverent.

"Watch him closely," Cornelius had said in a low voice then. "This is how a day should be lived - one meaningful motion at a time."

The clockmaker hadn't looked up when he'd said, "Forty-eight years I have worked with these gears."

Marius remembered asking, half-smiling, "Doesn't it become repetitive?"

The old craftsman had given a soft laugh. "Repetitive? My boy, I do not repair clocks. I repair time."

Those words now settled into Marius again like a tender warm stone in cold hands.

He remembered Cornelius stepping forward.

"Every man dreams of greatness," he had said, "but most ignore the small motions that hold the entire mechanism of life together. Break a single gear, and the whole clock stumbles. Repair the right one, and everything finds rhythm again."

He had signaled toward the tools arranged neatly on the bench.

"Purpose works the same way. A day is too long for a man who fills it with worry. But when a man fills it with intention - even a small intention - the day shrinks to a size the heart can carry."

The clockmaker had placed the restored watch on the counter.

"The smallest parts dictate the accuracy of the whole," he'd said. "One misaligned tooth can ruin the hour. One careful adjustment can restore perfect harmony."

Cornelius had glanced at Marius.

"Small choices shape the entire day," he had said. "People look for transformation in grand decisions, but it hides in quiet moments: rising when you'd rather lie down, forgiving when bitterness feels easier, pausing before reacting, choosing gratitude instead of complaint. These tiny acts balance the gears of the soul."

Then Cornelius had paused, as if remembering something age-old and relevant.

"This is the lesson Martha struggled to learn in the house at Bethany," he'd said.

"In **Luke 10:38–42**, Martha busied herself with every urgent task. She believed motion alone meant meaning. But Mary sat at the feet of Jesus, listening, unrushed, undistracted, centered. When Martha cried out in frustration, the answer was gentle: 'Mary has chosen what is better.'"

Cornelius had directed attention to the walls of ticking clocks around them.

"That is the clockmaker's secret," he'd said. "Two women. One house. Two choices. One focused on everything. One focused on the one thing that mattered. And focus - not frantic motion - is what transformed the moment."

"Routine without intention drains the spirit. Routine with meaning strengthens it. Mary wasn't idle - she was aligned. She adjusted the gear that controlled all the others."

Standing now on the sidewalk outside, Marius recognized that even the memory of that room seemed to slow time. The air in his mind felt still, almost sacred. The flow of time had behaved differently there - not as a taskmaster, but as something responsive to the quality of attention given to it.

He could almost feel Cornelius's warm, steady hand on his shoulder again.

"The day expands or contracts based on the heart that carries it," the old man had said. "When intention leads the hour, even repetition becomes holy. When purpose guides each step, the day no longer towers like a burden. It becomes manageable - meaningful - almost beautiful."

As he turned away from the shop now, Marius whispered the line Cornelius had left him with that day:

"The world does not brighten for the man who waits.

Daylight comes to the one who begins."

He walked on, understanding yet again:

A day is never too long when you fill it with purpose.

Too long only when left empty.

The Tyranny of Comparison

By late afternoon, the streets were crowded again. Marius watched people hurry by - better dressed, more confident, seemingly built from sturdier material. A young man with earbuds jogged past, smiling as if life itself had quietly murmured him a compliment. A businessman stepped into a sleek car. A couple laughed together around hot cups at a café table.

That old ache rose silently in his chest.

He knew this feeling too; he knew exactly how Cornelius had dealt with it before.

"Your eyes are drifting again," he felt as if he heard the old man say.

He thought back to the day they had been seated together on a bench while the city beat around them.

"It just feels like everyone else is ahead," Marius had admitted. "I'm trying, but…"

Cornelius had rested a hand on the back of the bench and motioned for him to sit fully, to stop moving for a moment.

"Let me ask you something," he had said. "Would you exchange your entire life - every joy you tasted, every lesson learned, every person who shaped you - for someone's story you only know from a distance?"

Marius had shaken his head. "No. I wouldn't."

"Then why envy a life you would never trade for?"

Cornelius had signaled toward the busy street.

"You see the lantern others carry," he'd said, "but not the load that bends their spine."

Silence had floated between them before he added:

"Comparison steals more energy than work ever will. A man may lift a heavy stone with strength, but he cannot take one step forward while envy anchors his feet."

He had leaned back, eyes tender but sharp with memory.

"Cain walked that road," he'd said quietly. "He stopped looking at his own offering and started staring at Abel's. He lost sight of the value of his own labor and poisoned his spirit with resentment. God warned him, 'Turn to doing good' **(Genesis 4:7)**. But comparison hollowed him from the inside."

Marius had felt the sting of that truth even then.

"Comparison rarely begins with envy," Cornelius had gone on. "It begins with exhaustion. A man grows weary of his journey and believes someone else's must be easier."

He gave a tender smile and narrated the story Jesus told about workers in a vineyard, found in **Matthew 20:1-16**.

"A landowner hired laborers at different times of the day but paid them all the same, sparking complaints from those who worked the whole day."

"But the early workers in the vineyard thought the same thing as Cain. Had the landowner paid them first, they would have gone home satisfied. Their joy collapsed only when they saw another man's blessing. Not the work. Not the wage. The comparison."

"A man can lose a lifetime of contentment in a single sideways glance," he had sighed.

Now, standing alone amid the crowd, Marius felt those words again.

"Listen closely, Marius," Cornelius's voice said deep inside him. "The man who compares his journey to another's will never know rest. He trades gratitude for grievance, contentment for craving, progress for paralysis. Envy dries the heart like heat on desert stone. But the man who focuses on his own path finds strength rising inside him like a quiet spring."

"You envy them," he had said once, pointing to strangers who looked composed and successful, "but you do not see their battles. The mother who looks confident may be drowning in quiet exhaustion. The businessman may be carrying debts heavier than your own. The young man who jogs with a smile may run to escape memories he cannot bear sitting still long enough to face."

"The world never tells the full story," Cornelius had reminded him. "You see the surface - never the sorrow underneath. You see the reward - never the wounds that earned it. You see outcomes - never the nights of fear, doubt, and trembling behind them."

"Your journey is sacred because it is yours," he had said, hand warm on Marius's shoulder. "Walking another man's path would undo you."

"Comparison is the thief of gratitude," he had added, "and gratitude is the mother of focus. Lose gratitude, and the day becomes too long. Keep gratitude, and even the heaviest day becomes light enough to carry."

Now, as the crowd ebbed and flowed around him, Marius lifted his face, just as Cornelius once had urged Cain to do in that ancient story.

He breathed deeply and silently thanked God for small, specific things that were his alone - the aged notebook in his bag, the lessons engraved in his core, the second chance of this very day.

He realized with a silent conviction:

He did not need another man's life.

He only needed to live his own - bravely, gratefully, steadily - one clear day at a time.

One Good Day

That night, back in his apartment, Marius opened his notebook once more. The words of the day, the memories of Cornelius's voice, the stitched-together lessons of years all seemed to converge on a single idea.

He remembered one of Cornelius's simplest invitations - one that had sounded almost too gentle to change a life, and bore the quiet force of a revolution.

"Live a single day so well," the old man had told him once on a busy city sidewalk, "that if the sun never rose again, you would feel no regret."

They had stood watching the morning crowd rush past with empty urgency - briefcases swinging, coffee tipping, brows furrowed by worries borrowed from a future not yet lived.

"Most people lose the day," Cornelius had murmured then, "not because they lack hours, but because their hearts never enter the morning. A day without intention becomes a day of reaction. And when a man reacts long enough, chance becomes his only master."

He had rested a hand on Marius's shoulder, steady and certain.

"One good day," he'd said, "has the power to redirect ten broken years."

Marius carried those words into many sunrises after that - including this one.

The mornings were not smooth. The coffee machine sometimes coughed. Trains were delayed. Tense messages tried to pull him back into old anxieties. But each time, he remembered the challenge, not to conquer the day, but to live it.

He paused.

He breathed.

He chose again.

He did not try to win the year, or the month, or even the week.

He tried to win the moment in front of him.

When irritation rose, he answered softly instead of sharply.

When his mind tried to scatter, he completed one meaningful task with full attention.

When discouragement whispered, he walked outside for a few minutes of light and reminded himself that he was still here, still breathing, still becoming.

When a stranger cut ahead of him in line, he let peace outrank pride.

When an old friend came to mind, he called, offering the encouragement he once believed he had none of.

And something impressive had found a foothold inside him.

By nightfall on those days, he felt quietly satisfied - not triumphant, not euphoric, but deeply firm as though the day had opened a small, sanctified spot where he finally lived within the hours instead of being chased by them.

He could still see Cornelius's approving smile in his mind.

"You understand now," the old man had said. "The beauty of one good day lies not in its perfection, but in its presence. A day lived with intention becomes a lantern for tomorrow."

Cornelius had compared it to the manna in the wilderness - a day's portion for a day's journey **(Exodus 16:4)**.

Strength for today, never for tomorrow. Grace measured to the moment. Peace is found only where the feet stand.

"A day is too long," he had said, "for a man whose mind wanders everywhere except the present. But when the heart settles into the hour, the day becomes light as bread from heaven."

Sitting in the calm now, Marius realized - again - that one good day has the power to heal the remains of a hundred wounded ones.

One good day could reignite a light he had thought time had smothered.

One good day could whisper:

You are still capable. You are still becoming.

He did not need flawless weeks.

He did not need perfect seasons.

He needed one good day - repeated with humble courage and quiet intention.

To live with resolve was to live awake.

To rise not asking, "Why me?" but declaring, "What now?"

To greet the morning as an opportunity, not a burden.

To shape the hours like clay, trusting that small strokes form the vessels of a life.

Life did not begin somewhere far ahead.

Life began here - in this breath, this choice, this sunrise entrusted to his care.

"This is the day that Jehovah has made; we will be joyful and rejoice in it."
— Psalm 118:24

A man who learns to command one day discovers a quiet mastery over time itself.

And as Cornelius had told him during one of their final walks together - a line that now resounded like an ending bell in his heart:

"The secret is not to make every day perfect. The secret is to make every day yours."

The lessons of intention had settled deeply into Marius's heart - presence, discipline, perspective, patience, the courage to choose again. They had become anchors strong enough to steady him through a thousand dawns.

But life has a way of testing the very truth a man has learned to love.

Sometimes the test comes gently, and sometimes it comes like a wave that darkens the sky without warning.

In the days ahead, Marius would discover that even a heart trained for intention can quiver when loss arrives suddenly at its door.

Yet those same lessons - the pause, the presence, the one good day - would become the rope that kept him steady when the ground beneath him moved slightly.

For the power acquired in calm mornings is never wasted.

It waits.

It gathers.

And when the tempest finally rises, that strength becomes the dawn a man did not know he would need.

Chapter Thirteen: The Longest Night-Finding Stability in Tragedy

❧

"All that I have taught you was never for the years ahead, but for the day before you. Grief is love searching for where to go."

— Cornelius.

"Weeping may come in the evening, but in the morning, there is a joyful cry."

— Psalm 30:5

"Jehovah is close to the brokenhearted; He saves those who are crushed in spirit."

— Psalm 34:18

The Call That Broke the Day in Two

The day did not begin as a tragedy.

It commenced like any other typical morning, and Marius had learned to respect. He rose before the alarm, sat on the edge of his bed, and let his feet find the cool floor.

He spoke quietly the words he had written at the top of so many pages now:

"Today will count."

He moved through his small apartment with quiet purpose.

Put water on for coffee.

Opened the window to let in the thin overcast light.

Reached for his notebook to write his three questions:

What matters most today?

Who can I help today?

What must I finish, no matter what?

His pen lingered over the page. For a strange moment, the questions seemed weightier than usual, as though the day on its own were holding its life force. He shook it off, wrote his answers, and moved to the kitchen.

The coffee machine coughed to life.

His phone rang.

He looked at the screen. It was Mrs. Alvarez - the woman who lived two doors down from Cornelius.

A small unease moved through him. He answered.

The sound of her voice arrived in pieces, shaking with the pace of her accent.

"Marius… have you heard?…I didn't know who else to call…"

The rest came in pieces his mind would later rearrange:

"Early this morning…"

"…didn't answer the door…"

"…we called an ambulance…"

"…they did what they could…"

Silence.

"He is gone, my dear. Cornelius is gone."

The moment hung in the air, defined by the fainter clink of his mug hitting the floor and shattering. It still carried the light scent of the spice-infused coffee Cornelius had introduced him to, a scent that now wafted through the room as softly as a hint of memory. Coffee spread in a dark bloom across the tile.

For a long moment, the single sound within the room was his own breathing, sharp, uneven, fighting the burden that had just dropped onto his chest.

The world outside went on as if nothing had happened: buses groaned, horns sounded, footsteps passed in the hallway. But inside Marius, something had gone completely, devastatingly still.

He did not remember grabbing his coat.

He did not remember crossing the street or climbing the hill.

Later, he would only recall the sensation of moving through a world that no longer seemed to belong to him.

When he reached Cornelius's building, the ambulance was gone.

The door was left partially open.

The Longest Walk

Mrs. Alvarez met him in the hallway, her eyes red, her hands twisting a dish towel she'd forgotten she was holding.

"They took him a little while ago," she uttered gently. "He… he went quietly. In his chair, by the window."

Marius nodded, though the words scarcely registered.

His legs bore him, almost of their own accord, toward the familiar door at the end of the corridor.

Cornelius's apartment was not empty - it was full of presence in the way only a recently vacated room can be.

The chair by the window still contained the shape of a man who had experienced many years in conversation with the dawn.

His cane rested against the side table.

His worn lantern sat near the bookshelf, as if waiting for another evening walk.

On the desk lay his notebook, open to a page half-filled with slanted, thoughtful handwriting.

The pen rested beside it, as though the sentence had only paused for breath.

The sight broke something inside Marius that took his knees with it.

He sank into the chair opposite the empty one and pressed his palms on his face.

No tears came at first. Merely an empty numbness, a ringing silence that rendered every sound in the room feel far away.

The old questions came rushing in - questions Cornelius had taught him to replace, questions that now returned with the force of a storm:

Why him?

Why now?

Why this way?

He had been prepared for many things - failure, delay, rejection, the slow grind of rebuilding a life one day at a time.

He had not been prepared for this.

The Longest Night

The hours that followed did not move in any way a clock could measure.

They stretched and folded, alternately frozen and rushing, like water caught between rock and gravity.

People came and went, the building superintendent, a quiet doctor with heavy eyes, a man from the congregation who spoke gently of arrangements and signatures. Mrs. Alvarez brought tea that had lost their warmth to the table.

Voices murmured. Papers were signed. Hands were shaken.

And through it all, Marius drifted like a man underwater, nodding when he was supposed to, answering when required, all while some part of him stood apart, stunned, watching the scene without believing it.

Eventually, the apartment emptied.

The sun dropped.

The city outside pulled its lights on like a suit of armor against the dark.

Marius found himself alone in Cornelius's study - a small room lined with books, quiet and warm, the same place where he had first seen the golden scar of the kintsugi cup.

Now the cup sat on the shelf, still gleaming, its fracture held together by light.

He rose slowly, took it down, and held it in both hands.

"This was once broken," Cornelius had said. "And someone decided the break was worthy of beauty."

The memory tightened his throat.

"Your cracks are not signs of unworthiness.

They are proof of survival.

Proof that you agreed to live again."

He thought of his own cracks - seasons of failure, relapse, disappointment, regret.

Cornelius had walked him through every one of them.

But who, he wondered now, could walk a man through the fracture of losing the one who taught him how to heal?

He moved to the window. The city's lights glowed hazily behind a thin film of unfallen tears.

For the first time since their earliest conversations, the night turned too long again.

Not because it lacked purpose, but because it appeared to extend ahead without the one voice that helped him name it.

Voices within the Silent Space

Grief has an odd way of summoning old words back to life.

As Marius stood there, holding the cup, he heard Cornelius everywhere - not in some mystical whisper, but in the persistent trace of memory, the way a house holds the sound of years.

"The unit of destiny is the day."

"Master one day, my boy. Treat the next sunrise as a gift, not a guarantee."

"A man's defeat is not written in the fall itself, but in his refusal to rise."

"The man who refuses to rise after falling has not failed; he has surrendered. But the one who stands again, though trembling, has already won."

Tonight, standing felt overwhelming.

He sank into Cornelius's chair - the very place the old man had taken his final breath - and let the heaviness of the moment settle onto his shoulders.

From somewhere deep within, an old impulse surfaced - the one that once drove him to drink, to run, to hide from anything that hurt too deeply.

Escape.

Numb this.

You don't have to feel all of it.

Another voice rose to meet it - quieter, but steadier.

"The secret, my boy, is not to stay unbroken.

It's to stay on the wheel."

He saw the potter's hands again, wet with clay, refusing to discard what had collapsed.

He heard the quiet buzz of the wheel.

He remembered.

Grief was not the moment to abandon the lessons.

Grief was the moment the lessons had been training him for.

The Night You Cannot Shorten.

Cornelius had earlier mentioned to him, "You cannot shorten every day by changing your circumstances. Some days you can only shorten by changing how you walk through them."

This night, Marius realized, was one of those days.

He could not negotiate with death.

He could not bargain with time.

He could not insist that this, of all days, be different.

But he could decide what this night would mean.

He opened Cornelius's notebook, the one that still lay on the desk. The last line, written in a script that wavered only slightly, read:

A man does not choose how long he lives, but he can decide how fully he lives the day entrusted to him.

No period.

No closing flourish.

Just a thought mid-stride.

Marius followed the words with his finger.

"Is this how it ends for everyone?" he uttered. "An unfinished sentence?"

He sat there a long time, breathing in the accustomed smell of weathered books and lamp oil. Slowly, something changed in his grief - not the disappearance of pain, but the faintest outline of purpose taking shape inside it.

He remembered another lesson:

"When you ask, 'Why me?' your gaze drops backward. But when a man asks, 'What now?' the road appears under his feet."

To help you operationalize this shift in perspective, consider pausing to contemplate your own journey. Think of a current setback or challenge you are facing and ask yourself, "What now?" Write your thoughts in a journaling box, focusing on the implementable measures and new possibilities this question reveals. By reframing the situation, you may discover a course ahead that you hadn't seen before.

His heart pained with the unfairness of it.

He wanted to rage.

He wanted to demand an explanation.

Instead, he uttered hoarsely into the quiet room:

"What now?"

The words trembled, but they were asked.

And inside that tiny question, the night shortened, not on the clock, though in the heart that had just shifted from helplessness to intention.

The Funeral and the Hidden Harvest

Cornelius's funeral was simple, just as he would have wanted it.

The hall was modest, sunlight shining through high windows, casting gentle rectangles on timeworn wooden pews, weathered sentinels of sorrow, as the soft voices of grief were absorbed, their surfaces polished by mourners' gentle touch. A handful of flowers rested near a framed photograph of the old man: eyes radiant, lines of cheer engraved deeply, the trace of a smile that knew more than it said.

Marius sat near the front, hands folded, the small stone from the hill and the smooth river pebble Cornelius once gave him tucked in his pocket.

As people stood to speak, Marius began to realize what he had only ever observed in fragments.

The blacksmith from the industrial quarter spoke first, his tone coarse with emotion.

"He used to visit the forge," he said. "Said the fire reminded him of the way life shapes men. He'd stand there watching for an hour, then leave me with one sentence that stayed in my head for days. I never met anyone who could see so much in a piece of metal."

The owner of the little café shared next.

"He'd sit in the corner, at the same table every Tuesday, and ask the barista how her exams were going. Not just 'How are you?' - he'd remember what you told him weeks before. When my father was ill, he was the only customer who noticed I'd been crying. He didn't give advice. He just said, 'Let the tears come. They are the proof you still care.'"

Mrs. Alvarez spoke about groceries carried up too many stairs, quiet prayers in the hallway, and songs sang softly beneath his breath as he fixed a broken door.

A young man Marius had never seen before narrated a story about almost ending his life on a bridge one winter night, and an old man with a lantern who had walked beside him until the urge passed.

"He didn't preach," the young man said. "He just listened. Then he said, 'Walk with me until your thoughts grow tired.' We walked for two hours. I never forgot that."

Story after story poured out - fragments of kindness, questions that healed, silences that held, one good day lived repeatedly in a hundred different lives.

Marius sat very still.

He thought of the clockmaker, the potter, the farmer, the woman with the flower shop, the weary executive in the elevator, the blind beggar on the roadside, the early workers in the vineyard, and Mary at the feet of Jesus.

Cornelius hadn't merely taught lessons.

He had lived them.

"The unit of destiny is the day."

Now Marius saw the harvest of those days laid out in front of him like a field in late sunlight.

Stability in the Shaking

That night, the city seemed altered.

Empty, somehow.

As though one of its quiet foundations had been removed.

Marius walked home slowly. The bench where they had first met was just a bench now. The garden where they had spoken under hanging lanterns seemed smaller without the man who once sat in its center like a rooted tree.

He reached his apartment, closed the door behind him, and leaned his head against it.

The temptation came again - that old, familiar urge to escape.

"You don't have to be strong tonight," the dark part of him whispered. "You've lost too much. You're allowed to fall apart."

Another voice rose to meet it - steady, unmistakable, stitched into him by years of repetition:

"Pause before you react. That pause is the hinge on which the entire day turns."

He stayed there, eyes closed, breathing slowly.

One breath.

Then another.

Then another.

The pause did not erase the grief.

It anchored him inside it.

He moved to the table, pulled his notebook toward him, and opened it to a clean page.

His hand tremored as he wrote the date.

The urge to write nothing - to let the day stand as a blank in protest - was strong.

Instead, through burning eyes, he wrote three words in deliberate ink:

"Begin again grieving."

He stared at the phrase for a long time. It felt wrong and right at the same time.

He heard Cornelius's voice in memory:

"Every transformation begins on the morning a man decides who he intends to be."

Who would he be now, in this new, unwelcome landscape?

He picked up his pen again and wrote:

Today, my intention is not to be strong.

I intend to be honest.

He let the tears come then - not as an enemy, but as evidence.

He wept for the man who had found him on a park bench and refused to leave him in his old life.

He wept for the questions he would never get to ask.

He wept for the comfort of that worn voice, for the soft lantern glow on winter evenings, for the steady presence that had grown into a kind of home.

He wept until the raging storm within ran out of words.

And beneath the pain, he felt something small though unmistakable:

He was still here. Not as a ghost, but his legacy.

The Rope in the Dark

In the subsequent days, grief did not behave politely.

It came in waves.

Some mornings, he woke with a surprising calm - able to make coffee, answer emails, help at the charity, even laugh briefly with someone who needed it.

Other mornings, the simple act of getting out of bed seemed like ascending out of a collapsed building.

Yet through each day, something kept holding.

It was not a denial.

It was not numbness.

It was the rope Cornelius had been embedding within his life all along.

The law of the day.

The mirror and the window.

The compass and the clock.

The discipline of the pause.

The courage to begin again.

The choice to ask, not "Why me?" but "What now?" was necessary for Marius.

It was at such times of deep sorrow that another question emerged to guide him through the darkness: "Which value can still guide you tonight?" This basic question helped Marius identify his guiding principle, his personal north star in the midst of grief - a torch that provided him with agency and clarity when it seemed as if all else was fading.

But he reached for them, one by one, like handholds in a dark stairwell.

When anger rose, at God, at fate, at the cruelty of an existence that would take a man like Cornelius and leave lesser ones untouched - Marius paused.

Anger did not vanish.

But it did not own him.

When the day appeared too long again, he remembered:

"A day is too long for the man who drags tomorrow into it.

But a day becomes bearable when you give it only what it can carry."

So, he stopped trying to survive the rest of his life without Cornelius.

He focused on surviving - and living - one sunrise without him.

Then another.

Then another.

When comparison whispered - when he saw men laughing with their fathers, older mentors walking beside younger ones - he remembered:

"A man can lose a lifetime of contentment in a single sideways glance."

So, he brought his gaze back to his own path, his own pain, his own portion of grace.

Slowly, the long nights shortened.

Not because the hours changed.

But because his footing within them grew steadier.

Where Faith Meets Loss

Grief drew Marius into stories he had read many times but never needed until now.

He thought of Mary and Martha, standing before the tomb of their brother Lazarus - caught between heartbreak and a sliver of trembling hope.

He remembered that Jesus wept with them, not distant, not aloof, but deeply moved. He stood next to them in grief before He called the dead to rise.

That story - once an ancient miracle - has taken on a far more intimate truth for Marius:

Love is stronger than loss. Loss is not the final chapter.

Hope hints that the grave does not bind life, Marius remembered another of Cornelius' favorite scriptures, 'Your dead will live." — **Isaiah 26:19.**

Cornelius had often said:

"Faith is not blind optimism.

Faith is the quiet agreement between you and eternity that what was loved is never lost."

Those words steadied him, but grief quietly spoke its own quiet questions.

It occurred in one of those evenings - the kind when sorrow sits beside you like an old companion - that Marius rediscovered another passage he once skimmed without much thought:

"For the living know that they will die, but the dead know nothing at all…their love and their hate and their jealousy have already perished…they no longer have any share in what is done under the sun."— **Ecclesiastes 9:5, 6.**

The words touched him gently, not harshly - a kind of truth that clarified, not fear.

Cornelius was gone from the earth he once walked in.

Gone from the heaviness of sadness.

Gone from the exhaustion of living.

Gone away from the pain that had marked his final days.

And upon that realization, Marius found a surprising peace:

Cornelius no longer suffered.

No longer worried.

No longer carried the burdens of the living.

His journey under the sun had ended.

And that, too, held mercy.

Scripture continued:

"Whatever your hand finds to do, do it with all your might, for there is no work nor planning nor knowledge nor wisdom in the Grave, where you are going." **— Ecclesiastes 9:10**

These words did not crush him.

They awakened him.

If the dead no longer share in life's movements, then every act of love, every kindness, every purpose must be carried out now - while breath remains.

Grief, when seen through this lens, did not paralyze him. It pushed him forward.

Sowing in Sorrow

He opened his notebook and wrote the words that Cornelius had quoted many times and that now had become his lifeline:

"The one who watches the wind will not sow, and the one who looks at clouds will not reap." — **Ecclesiastes 11:4**

He finally understood:

The man who waits for a painless life will never plant anything worth harvesting.

Faith means sowing even when the sky is dark.

Believing that buried pain may bloom unseen.

Trusting that grief, too, has a season and a harvest.

He remembered another promise that Cornelius often mentioned:

"The righteous will inherit the earth and live upon it forever." **— Psalm 37:29**

"Blessed are the meek, for they shall inherit the earth." **— Matthew 5:5**

These truths did not erase the pain.

But they gave it direction.

A path.

A horizon.

The Nature of Tragedy

Cornelius's voice returned to him often:

"Pain is the doorway through which wisdom enters. The heart that refuses pain also refuses depth."

So Marius stopped resisting the pain.

He let grief carve space in him, not to break him, but to make him larger.

He came to understand tragedy not as a cruel interruption, but as a violent rearranging of what he had taken for granted. The world was no longer what it had been before Cornelius's death, and neither was he.

When happiness had made his life wide, grief was making it deep.

The Tree and the Roots

He returned often to the aged oak, the one that had lost a branch years before. Cornelius once showed it to him and said:

"The wound did not weaken the tree.

It expanded the roots."

Now, standing alone, Marius rested his hand on the scarred bark and whispered:

"Then let my roots deepen too."

The tree taught him something real:

Grief does not destroy when met with meaning.

Loss becomes soil.

What had appeared as pure tearing began, slowly, to feel as sowing seeds - painful, yes, still purposeful.

Kintsugi of the Heart

Late one night, he remembered a story Cornelius loved:

A potter dropped his most beautiful vessel. Rather than discarding it, he repaired it with gold dust and resin. When the sun struck the repaired cracks, the vessel gleamed brighter than before.

Cornelius called it "the resurrection of the ordinary."

The memory steadied him.

His heart would carry a crack now.

But perhaps the crack would shine.

He began writing letters - not to people, but to life itself.

Letters of gratitude, of confession, of desire, of hope.

He found that grief, honestly expressed, becomes a prayer the heart understands.

The Illusion of Strength

There was a time when Marius believed strength came from control - predicting, preventing, preparing for every possible outcome.

Now he wrote:

"The earth spins without my permission.

The sun rises without my command.

My peace must rest on what cannot be taken."

And so each morning, he prayed:

"Teach me to stand steady, even when the world moves."

Slowly, he did.

His strength was no longer the tight, brittle strength of a man trying to hold everything together. It was the quieter strength of someone who had learned to let some things go - especially the things no human heart was ever meant to carry alone.

The Subtle Whisper That Stayed

In his quietest moments, he sometimes felt Cornelius close - not as memory alone, but as presence in a distance.

"Look ahead, not beneath," the voice would softly utter.

"Stare too long at what is broken,

and you forget the shore you're walking toward."

And so he practiced seeing differently - not just the crevices in life, but the continuity beneath them.

Perspective became the bridge that carried him out of sorrow and into peace.

Stillness as Trust

During an evening, watching the sea mirror the fading sky, he wrote:

"Life is calculated not in years, but in awakenings.

I once believed meaning came from what I could build.

Now I know it rises from what I can notice."

He remembered another verse that Cornelius often quoted:

"Give in and know."**— Psalm 46:10**

Calmness was not emptiness.

Calmness was trust.

He no longer dreaded calm moments.

They became the place where grief and faith could sit together without rushing to resolve each other.

Becoming the Lantern

A certain evening, months after the funeral, Marius returned to the park where it had all begun. The bench was still there, overlooking the thin strip of grass and the tempo of the city beyond.

He sat down, hands in his pockets, noticing the usual roughness of the smooth stone and the small hill pebble between his fingers. The sky was the color of cooling embers.

People passed - hurried, tired, laughing, absorbed in thought. Faces he would never know. Stories he would never read.

And then Marius noticed someone he had seen only in passing - a young man who carried by a kind of practiced heaviness, as if carrying more than his years should allow.

For a moment, the young man walked by without looking up.

Then something amid the hush tugged him sideways, as though the burden on his shoulders needed somewhere to land.

“Excuse me,” he spoke quietly, “is it okay if I sit here?”

Marius nodded, shifting slightly to make room.

They sat in silence for a long minute, watching the lights blink on across the city. Finally, the young man exhaled - a sound halfway between a sigh and surrender.

"My name's Shawn," he whispered softly. "I'm… just tired. Not sleepy. Just tired of everything."

Marius turned, studying him gently.

Shawn's voice bore the strain of someone older than his age - the voice of a man who had been standing in the gap long before he felt ready. His shoulders were narrow but held like a shield, his eyes alert in the way of someone who had learned to protect others before himself.

He continued, voice unsteady:

"My dad left when I was ten. My little sister was only five. Mom worked two jobs for years - cleaning offices at night, and working as a cashier in the morning. She just… wore herself out trying to keep us going."

He swallowed.

"She passed last year. So now it's just my sister and me. I pick up whatever shifts I can, try to make sure she eats, tries her homework, and stays out of trouble. I've been grinding so long I don't even know what normal feels like anymore."

The confession came out fractured, halting, raw pieces of a life stitched together by exhaustion.

The old impulse rose: to reach for the perfect sentence, the exact formula, the polished wisdom Cornelius might have used.

Instead, he remembered Cornelious' sayings and the scripture he often quoted along with it:

"The man who lives by the compass doesn't always need to speak first. He needs only to be fully present."

"Be quick to listen, slow to speak."**— James 1:19**

Marius listened.

Deeply listened.

The way someone at one time had listened to him.

He perceived a tug of recognition - as if looking into a younger version of himself, standing on the edge of the same darkness he once knew too well.

When Shawn finished, Marius did not hand out quick fixes.

He did not try to fix what could not be repaired in a single moment.

"I don't know all the right words," he said humbly. "But I know what it's like for a night to feel endless."

Shawn looked at him - bewilderment and a thin, trembling ray of hope glowing beneath the exhaustion.

"What does that even mean, sir?" Shawn asked.

Marius thought of Cornelius's study, the forge, the potter's wheel, the clockmaker's bench, the shoreline at daybreak.

He thought of failure, hope, the long nights that once broke him - and the man who taught him how to shorten a day that seemed intolerable.

He spoke gently:

"It means the night only feels endless until you live one hour well inside it."

Shawn frowned slightly, trying to understand.

Marius continued, voice steadfast:

"Someone once told me to live a single day so well that if the sun never rose again, I wouldn't feel regret. Just one day. Not the whole future. Not the whole burden. One good day."

Shawn stared at the ground, absorbing it slowly.

For the first time since he sat down, the young man's shoulders lowered a bit - not relief, not escape, but the beginning of breath.

Marius turned toward him.

"You don't have to fix everything at once. Just one hour well lived. One choice made with intention. That's how the night begins to shorten."

They remained seated side by side until the street lamps buzzed fully awake.

When they finally rose, Shawn's posture was still tired - but not defeated.

A change had occurred.

As the young man walked away, Marius experienced a warmth stir inside him - quiet, steady, familiar.

Without realizing exactly when it had happened, he had begun carrying a lantern of his own.

And without knowing it yet, Shawn and his sister would one day become a portion of a journey far larger than this moment - an expedition that would unfold in a future chapter of Marius's life, and in a story yet to be written, when life makes no sense.

A New Rhythm of the Day

Years softened mourning into something gentler - a pain that taught rather than tore.

Each morning, Marius practiced shortening the day:

What deserves my time today?

Who can I bless before sunset?

What must I complete with peace in my heart?

He discovered something startling:

By giving himself wholly to a few meaningful things, his days became deeper, fuller, almost longer, though the hours never changed.

Cornelius had been right:

"The shorter the day, the fuller the life."

Grief held once made every hour feel empty.

Now, intention made every hour feel counted.

Passing the Torch Forward

Marius began sharing his mentor's wisdom quietly and humbly, just as it had been given to him.

Not with speeches, but with questions:

What can you do today that will make tomorrow lighter?

Who can you forgive before nightfall?

What simple deed could bring peace to your own heart?

He watched faces soften.

He saw hearts rekindle.

Cornelius's wisdom lived on - not through blood, but through heart.

Each time Marius saw someone straighten their shoulders, inhale with calm, or write their own "Today will count" at the top of a page, he felt something holy pass through the room:

A torch changing hands, a calm life at a time.

Practice: Walking Through Your Own Longest Night

If you are reading this with your own grief pressing on your chest - whether you have lost a person, a dream, a season of life, or an aspect of yourself you can't get back - this chapter is not just Marius's story. It is a beckoning.

You cannot rush grief.

But you can walk with it.

Here is a simple practice you can return to, again and again, on the nights that feel too long:

Name the loss honestly.

Sit somewhere quiet. With pen and paper, complete this sentence without censoring yourself:

"What I lost is…"

Write until the page feels heavy. Let your heart speak plainly.

Allow the tears, or the dryness.

If tears come, let them; if they don't, don't force them. Both are normal. Grief has many faces: tears, silence, fatigue, irritability, numbness. All are ways the heart says, "This mattered to me."

Ask Cornelius's question: not "Why me?" but "What now?"

When the "Why me?" rises - and it will - gently add a second question beside it:

"In honor of what I lost, what now?"

The answer may be small: get out of bed, drink water, make one phone call, forgive one thing, light one candle, write one line: "Today will count."

Shorten the day.

Instead of trying to survive the whole future, bring it back to one sunrise:

What is one gentle task I can do today?

Who is one person I can let in on how I really feel?

What can I lay down that I was never meant to carry alone?

Create a simple routine of remembrance.

Read some of Cornelius' favorite scriptures at the same time each week.

Walk a path they loved.

Keep one object - a stone, a note, a photo - and hold it while you breathe a simple line:

"You are gone from my sight, but not from my heart."

Anchor yourself in stillness.

Take one minute - just sixty seconds - to sit in silence and breathe slowly.

With each breath in, think: "I am still here."

With each breath out, think: "Teach me to stand steady, even when the world moves."

End the day with one sentence.

Before sleep, write a single line, even if it is only:

"I made it through today."

Over the course of days, you'll see something you may not feel yet: you are still moving. You are still becoming.

This is not a formula to fix pain.

It is a rope for the dark - the same rope Cornelius placed in Marius's hands, now quietly offered into yours.

Closing Words of the Chapter

That night, back in his apartment, Marius opened his notebook once more.

He wrote:

"Today did not erase the grief.

But it proved that grief cannot erase the gift."

He thought of Cornelius - of his chair, his lamp, his soft urgency in their final lessons.

He softly spoke into the dark:

"You are gone. But you are not gone from me."

Outside, the city carried on with its usual noise. Inside, the room had a different silence - not empty, but full.

He closed his eyes and remembered one last sentence, spoken on one of their final walks together:

"The secret is not to make every day perfect.

The secret is to make every day yours."

Marius inhaled slowly.

"This day was mine," he said. "And I gave it what I had."

He turned off the lamp.

The night remained quietly long.

The pain was still real.

But the surface below him no longer seemed like it was falling apart.

Chapter Fourteen: The New Dawn - When All Lessons become One

❧

"The sunrise that ends the night is the same light that began it."

— Cornelius.

"Write it on your heart that every day is the best day in the year."

— Ralph Waldo Emerson.

"The One who started a good work in you will bring it to completion until the day of Christ Jesus."

— Philippians 1:6

Marius stood once more below the oak.

The bench had aged gracefully now, its grain silvered by years of rain and sun, yet it seemed more alive than ever, as though memory itself had grown firm beneath it.

He closed his eyes and listened.

There was no voice, no sound of slow footsteps behind him, no familiar hand resting on his shoulder.

And yet - Cornelius was there.

Not in body, but in everything he had become.

Every word, every moment of pause, every truth the old man had previously spoken was now part of Marius's personal heartbeat.

He smiled quietly as he walked back to his apartment, realizing that the lessons never focused on the future at all.

They were about this - the day before him.

He remembered how it began - the confusion, the exhaustion, the burden of a man carrying too many yesterdays and too many tomorrows at once.

Life unfolded as a storm of unfinished thoughts and unhealed disappointments until Cornelius had said:

"You are trying to lift eternity, my boy. Shorten your day."

That was the key.

Not to stretch the hours thinner, but to live them more profoundly.

And so, Marius had come to understand life differently.

He learned that a single hour cherished deliberately is more valuable than a lifetime spent in distraction.

He learned that peace is not found in fixing the world, but in commanding the hour before you.

He had fought the endless battle of the mind and discovered that thoughts design destiny.

He had fallen and risen again, understanding that failure is never final - it is simply unfinished success.

He had learned to distinguish between worry and thought, to stop rocking in the chair of anxiety and start walking in the strength of faith.

He had learned that purpose is not invented - it is remembered.

That the Creator's words continue to whisper in human hearts: "Let there be light."

And when storms came, he stopped waiting for the clouds to clear; he worked while the wind blew, knowing that no harvest comes to the man who only watches the sky.

He learned that resilience is born not in calm but in fire, that the hand which wounds is also the hand that shapes.

He discovered that courage as well as persistence are the twin engines of all progress - that victory belongs not to the strongest, but to the one who refuses to stop striking the ground.

He learned the sacred power of friendship - that we become like those we walk with.

That joy grows among encouragers, while despair breeds in the company of the bitter.

He learned to change his vision, to adjust his lens when life blurred before him, and to take action even when he could not see the whole road ahead.

And when loss came, as it always does, he uncovered purpose in memory, strength in gratitude, and hope in the promise that love cannot die.

Then came intention.

The art of living each day as a discipline, a sacred task.

He began to live not by the clock, but by the compass - not measuring hours, but harmonizing them with purpose.

He learned that simplicity is power, that quietness is clarity, that joy lives in the present moment.

And when Cornelius was gone, the vacuum became its own teacher.

Through grief, he discovered stability - the peace that does not depend on circumstances but grows from understanding.

He learned that faith is balance, that tragedy refines the soul, and that even absence can be filled with presence.

Marius learned something more, unexpectedly, on the morning he stepped into the new season of his life.

It came quietly, as most revelations do, not in a flare of inspiration, but in a silent dawn that touches a window and reminds a man that he has survived the night.

He stood at his living room window, watching the early light stretch over the rooftops. The city was waking up, but it appeared changed now - not louder, not softer, simply… deeper. As if each sound carried purpose, and each breath carried instruction.

He found himself quietly uttering what he once heard from Cornelius under the aged oak:

"Each sunrise is mercy in motion."

At first, he had not understood. But now the meaning revealed like a slow-blooming flower. Every lesson, every moment, every scar, every breath had led him here - to this new beginning that didn't feel like a beginning at all, but like the unveiling of something that had forever been waiting.

The day looked steady in his hands.

Cornelius's memories no longer stung. They warmed him. They steadied him. They stood next to him like a faithful companion. And as he prepared a small cup of tea - something he had picked up from the old man's quiet rituals - he discerned a presence, not of sorrow, but of continuance. A thoughtful indication that grief does not take away love. If anything, it enlarges it.

He moved outdoors and walked to the small hill overlooking the city. The breeze was cool. The world radiated amber. And there, standing in the calm of morning, Marius realized something he had never before dared to see:

He was no longer the student who waited for guidance.

He had become the man who lived it.

Every lesson Cornelius had given - every story, every question, every moment of silence - had flowed into one truth, one core, one unshakeable principle:

A day is too long only when a man tries to live the whole of it at once.

But a day becomes beautiful - even everlasting - when lived one intention, one breath, one step at a time.

He thought of all the times when he had changed him:

The hour he learned to shorten the day.

The moment he faced failure, he did not collapse.

The pauses that taught him mastery.

The victories that came quietly, almost unnoticed.

The grief that engraved a new depth in him.

The sunrise that reminded him of eternity.

The love that outlived loss.

All moments were their own day.

Each day has its own life.

And all of them were leading him here - to the grasping that life itself was not assessed by years, but by awakenings.

He closed his eyes, and briefly, Cornelius's voice came back as clearly as if the old man stood next to him:

"When all lessons become one, the day becomes everlasting."

The words rested softly into Marius's bones.

He breathed.

He smiled.

And in that calm morning, he perceived a rare, unshakable peace.

He had ultimately understood how to live.

And now, dear reader, the story that molded Marius reaches your hands like a lantern passed from one traveler to the next. Perhaps you see yourself somewhere in these pages - in the questions he asked, in the fears he faced, in the losses he carried, in the beginnings he held back to make.

Perhaps you are the one standing between yesterday and tomorrow, unsure of how to move, uncertain of how to breathe, doubtful whether the light ahead belongs to you.

If so, hear this gently:

You have more strength than you believe.

More hope than you feel.

More future than your present suggests.

Whatever you have lost - a loved one, a dream, a relationship, a season of life - none of it was wasted. Grief may bend you, but it does not erase you. Pain may interrupt your path, but it cannot cancel your purpose.

All setbacks have been shaping your roots.

Every tear has been watering something unseen.

Every night has been preparing you for a dawn that carries your name.

You may feel as though you've been living in fragments, but those fragments are pieces of a larger story - a tale that progresses, that deepens, that strengthens with each day you refuse to surrender.

Marius did not rise because life became easy.

He rose because he learned the rhythm of the day.

And now you can too.

Start with one good morning.

One intention.

One pause.

One step that says, “I am still here.”

Start with the truth that carried him through loss:

The God who watched over yesterday also watches today, and tomorrow rests in His hands.

The unchanged voice that called Lazarus from the tomb still calls the weary to rise.

The same promise that carried Mary, Martha, Joseph, David, Job -

still carries anyone brave enough to trust it.

Even now, even here, even you.

Do not wait until the entire map loads before you move.

Do not wait for perfect clarity or understanding before you begin.

Do not wait for the world to make sense before you trust that God is still speaking.

Life will not always give answers - but it always gives a day.

And the day you hold in your hands is not a burden.

It is a gift.

A clean sheet.

A beginning.

A call to rise.

This is the everlasting day - the day when all the lessons become one,

when each difficulty forms a single wisdom,

when every breath becomes a step toward purpose.

Live this day. Own this day. Shape this day. And as you do, remember this:

Shorten today by focusing on one intention and taking one pause. Transform inspiration into practice with a single, actionable step. And tomorrow will bow to your courage.

As you close this book, you are not ending the journey.

You are beginning a deeper one, a journey into the questions on the far side of the horizon, the unknowns that mold our pain and guide our hope, the answers that speak softly in the teeth of adversities of life.

And when the world does not make sense, as it often won't - there is a voice that still speaks.

A voice as steady as daybreak, as gentle as mercy, as clear as truth.

That voice has more to tell you.

The following sunrise holds a conversation waiting for your heart.

And so the next chapter of your life begins...

When Life Does Not Make Sense: What God Told You.

The day is yours now.

Go and live it well.

Final Resolution

Before you close this book, pause for a moment, not to remember every line, but to claim what the story has been trying to place gently into your hands.

Marius's change was never meant to feel like a dramatic rescue. It was meant to feel like something truer: a return to steadiness. A return to the present. A return to the part of life you can actually hold. Again and again, the lesson was simple, but not shallow: the day becomes unbearable when you try to live all of it at once - yesterday's grief, today's pressure, and tomorrow's fear stacked into a single breath. But the day becomes livable - even meaningful - when you shorten it on purpose and give it one clear aim.

If you are finishing this book with a quiet heaviness still in your chest, you are not reading it wrong. Some burdens do not vanish because a chapter ends. Some pain remains present even after wisdom arrives. But what can change - starting now - is how you carry it. You can stop treating your life as a problem you must solve in one sitting. You can stop demanding clarity before movement. You can learn to walk with what you don't yet understand, and still be faithful to what you *do* know: that you have this day, this breath, this moment - and you are allowed to begin from here.

So here is a closing practice, offered to you the way Cornelius offered everything - quietly, without pressure, but with conviction:

When you wake, don't ask, "How do I fix my whole life?"
Ask, "What is the one thing that matters most **today**?"

Write it down. Make it small enough to finish, meaningful enough to matter.

Then guard your mind like a doorway. Not everything deserves entry. Not every fear deserves rehearsal. When worry tries to rock you in place, name it for what it is - movement without progress - and return to one action you can take now. The day doesn't ask you to be perfect. It asks you to be present.

And when you fail - and you will, in some way - do not use it as proof that you are hopeless. Use it as evidence that you are human and still learning. You are not disqualified because you stumbled. You are shaped because you stood again. Healing is not a straight path. It is often a quiet series of returns: returning to your intention, returning to your faith, returning to the next right step.

There will be mornings when you feel strong, and mornings when you feel like you are beginning all over again. On the hardest days, let this be enough: one pause, one honest prayer, one small act of order, one phone call you've been avoiding, one apology, one glass of water, one walk outside, one page read, one task completed, one decision not to quit. Do not despise the smallness of what you can do. Small faithfulness rebuilds lives.

Because this is the deeper truth the story leaves with you: purpose is not something you find only at the finish line. Purpose is what you practice in the middle - when the bills are real, when grief still visits, when the future is unclear, when the world does not slow down for your pain. It is choosing, again and again, to live this day with intention instead of letting it live you.

So as you step away from these pages, don't think of it as an ending. Think of it as a handoff.

The lantern has been placed in your hands now. Not to light the entire road at once - only the next few steps.

Shorten the day.

Choose one intention.

Take one brave action.

Let the next sunrise meet you moving.

"The day is yours now. Go and live it well."

Epigraph

"Teach us how to count our days, so that we may acquire the heart of wisdom.

— Psalm 90:12

"A day is too long only when it is lived without intention."

— Cornelius.

www.ingramcontent.com/pod-product-compliance
Ingram Content Group UK Ltd.
Pitfield, Milton Keynes, MK11 3LW, UK
UKHW060116010826
14089UKWH00003B/17

9 798902 241317